What Pe[illegible]

MW01182276

With Halftime- Learning to Pivot as a Leader and Identifying Your Next Step, *Adrian Bracy has given us a wonderful gift—the gift of deeply grounded encouragement and a new challenge. Her foundational faith in God and His provision is contagious!*

Adrian has the singular voice of a Black woman who led as a senior executive in the NFL, then pivoted to a calling to advance racial equity in a new way and inspire women throughout her life. She touches all of us deeply! Serving in spaces where most leaders don't look like Adrian, or like me, I have a deep gratitude to God that He has raised up Adrian to show us how to pause, to take a half time, and sense where God is working in very practical ways—and then to lean into our passion with resilience.

This book will make you gently uncomfortable and inspire you to think about the pivots in your own life. You will be touched by Adrian's life story, and her engaging and infectious faith that drives her purpose.

David L. Steward
Founder and Chairman, World Wide Technology
Author of *Doing Business by the Good Book* and *Leadership by the Good Book*

As we grow through life, there will invariably be times when we come to a crossroads of change. Adrian refers to seasons like these as our half-times. She not only shares her own half-time stories with us, but she encourages us to be highly aware of our own gut responses, to seek the wisdom of trusted advisors, and most importantly, to listen to the voice of God as we navigate changes in our lives. Adrian shows us through her stories that pivoting in life is not only OK, but can even be times to relish. A half-time surrendered to a loving and all-knowing God will guide us to living our best lives now.

Lisa Nichols, CEO, Technology Partners

HALFTIME

Learn to Pivot as a Leader and Identify Your Next Step

Best Wishes,
Adrian

ADRIAN ELIZABETH BRACY

EMBRACE PUBLISHING

HALFTIME

Learn to Pivot as a Leader and Identify Your Next Step
Adrian Elizabeth Bracy
Embrace Publishing

Published by Embrace Publishing, St. Louis, MO
Copyright ©2021 Adrian Elizabeth Bracy
All rights reserved.

No part of this publication may be reproduced, stored in a retrieval system, or transmitted in any form or by any means, electronic, mechanical, photocopying, recording, scanning, or otherwise, except as permitted under Section 107 or 108 of the 1976 United States Copyright Act, without the prior written permission of the Publisher. Requests to the Publisher for permission should be addressed to Permissions Department, Embrace Publishing, embrace@adrianbracy.com.

Limit of Liability/Disclaimer of Warranty: While the publisher and author have used their best efforts in preparing this book, they make no representations or warranties with respect to the accuracy or completeness of the contents of this book and specifically disclaim any implied warranties of merchantability or fitness for a particular purpose. No warranty may be created or extended by sales representatives or written sales materials. The advice and strategies contained herein may not be suitable for your situation. You should consult with a professional where appropriate. Neither the publisher nor author shall be liable for any loss of profit or any other commercial damages, including but not limited to special, incidental, consequential, or other damages.

Editor: Kay Clark-Uhles

Cover and Interior design: Davis Creative, DavisCreative.com

Publisher's Cataloging-In-Publication Data
(Prepared by The Donohue Group, Inc.)

Names: Bracy, Adrian Elizabeth, author.
Title: Halftime : learn to pivot as a leader and identify your next step / Adrian Elizabeth Bracy.
Description: St. Louis, MO : Embrace Publishing, [2021] | Includes bibliographical references.
Identifiers: ISBN 9798985030105 (paperback) | ISBN 9798985030129 (hardback) | ISBN 9798985030112 (ebook)
Subjects: LCSH: Leadership. | Bracy, Adrian Elizabeth. | Organizational change. | Change (Psychology) | Teams in the workplace. | Success in business. | BISAC: BUSINESS & ECONOMICS / Leadership. | BUSINESS & ECONOMICS / Women in Business. | SELF-HELP / Personal Growth / General.
Classification: LCC HD57.7 .B73 2021 (print) | LCC HD57.7 (ebook) | DDC 658.4092--dc23

ATTENTION CORPORATIONS, UNIVERSITIES, COLLEGES AND PROFESSIONAL ORGANIZATIONS: Quantity discounts are available on bulk purchases of this book for educational, gift purposes, or as premiums for increasing magazine subscriptions or renewals. Special books or book excerpts can also be created to fit specific needs. For information, please contact Embrace Publishing, embrace@adrianbracy.com.

Table of Contents

Foreword

As an NFL head football coach, you are always looking for leadership support within your organization, hoping to find people you can share your responsibilities as a leader with as you implement your vision, values, and process. Fortunately for me, Adrian Bracy was one of the individuals working at the other end of the building, willing to step up and get emotionally involved in rebuilding the losing-est NFL franchise in the league!

Granted, Adrian was not a football coach; she was vice president of finance, a totally separate division of the St. Louis Rams organization. But have finances ever not been important to the success of any business, regardless of what type of business you are in? The proper use of funds has always been a significant contributor to success when it is invested in what helps a team win. Adrian made sure this took place.

Adrian and I first met when I became the head football coach of the St. Louis Rams in 1997. She had been there for two years, so she had experienced a few of the down years and was very willing to get involved in the rebuilding process that I, along with my assistant coaching staff, was about to install. Even though we worked at the opposite ends in the building, we became united by one goal: turn the Rams into a world champion organization in every department.

It didn't take me long to recognize Adrian was going to be a real positive contributor to my overall philosophical approach to leading.

One of my first challenges was to re-unite the organization emotionally. The people in the building had been demoralized by the accumulation of losing seasons! Fortunately for me, I found an immediate ally in Adrian Bracy.

When a common mission is initiated within every department in a building, the rebuilding process comes together much faster. Adrian, with her everlasting smile, took on the mission of morale improvement, utilizing her innate talents as a leader to sell our vision, values, process, and relationship-building programs! This is not easy to do when you know the first year or two may not be successful, win/loss wise, so all your leaders must know how to properly handle the adversity that accompanies losing. Using failure as a motivator isn't easy, but we all did, including Adrian. When problems become your ally, you have a real chance to succeed! We just didn't allow the initial losing seasons to define who we were. We remained positive, attacked the problems, not our people, and kept on working!

I appreciated everyone's personal contribution to rebuilding the Rams into a world-champion Super Bowl team in the three-year time period that we got it done. It is very difficult to do. The teams that had been winning all along don't sit back and allow complacency to overtake them; they work harder to remain in the position they had gained as a result of their hard work, so your leadership team has to be a great one.

Adrian's contribution to the team was more than a contribution to the team's success; she made a difference! Her caring attitude about her responsibilities and the people she worked with was infectious; consequently, they cared about her as well and our team goals! The examples she set as the leader in her department permeated the attitudes of all her fellow workers. Somewhere along the way she recognized her team would not be what she wasn't. She had well-defined articulated plans that were easy for her staff to understand and believe in; therefore, they trusted her process. The relationships within her department while going through adversity were strengthened because of how well she handled them; then when we started winning, these relationships really became close. All a reflection of a really good leader.

One other real attribute I really appreciated about Adrian's leadership style was her work ethic. When the boss works hard, so does the rest of the team. Again, somewhere along the line, she recognized hard work was not a form of punishment; it was her solution! Maybe developed by her early childhood experiences, but yet another positive example.

Everything I've tried to express within this foreword can be substantiated by reading Adrian's book. Having already read the unedited copy, I think you will believe, as I did, and still do, her innate self-developed leadership qualities are a reflection of a sincere person with great integrity who really wants to try to make a positive difference in the lives of people!

Dick Vermeil, Retired NFL Coach

Preface

Here we are, August 2021, amid a pandemic and I'm writing a book on leadership. This all sounds so unbelievable to me. If I had completed my book when I first had the desire in 2017, it would have been a totally different book. Back then, I started writing an autobiography but it seemed too boring. In hindsight, I'm glad I waited until now.

It wasn't until 2018 that I knew I was at halftime in a career spanning forty years working for other people and that I wanted a new chapter in life, coaching leaders and public speaking. In football, halftime allows the coach and team to pivot or make adjustments in the second half. In business and personal lives, halftime is the same—except that we have the opportunity for multiple halftimes in our lives. We get to stop and take time to evaluate our careers or life to see what's working, what's not, and make adjustments, or pivot in another direction, which is what I did several times in my career. So I knew it was time to pivot to entrepreneurship in 2018.

I have volunteered as a women's mentor and coach for decades because it's my passion, and I decided why not make a living on something about which I'm passionate. I've also done a ton of speaking engagements at no cost, so why not get paid for sharing my wisdom—after all, as a servant leader, I enjoy helping others reach their fullest potential. I have had the experience of working in the NFL for nearly eighteen years, as CEO of a nonprofit for nearly twelve years, and in various accounting positions nine years prior to the NFL, so I have a lot of wisdom to share. And in my opinion, and with my faith, I am obliged to do so.

I hope this book will give you some encouragement that you have all you need to succeed in life; you only have to ask, receive, and activate your faith in God and yourself.

The pandemic has required most of us to pivot one way or another. My halftime experiences throughout my career taught me the meaning of "pivot" and how to embrace the change.

In this book, I expose my vulnerabilities in hopes they will give you the courage to follow your dreams and reach the stars.

Wishing you all the best,

Adrian

Acknowledgments

I won't kid you writing this book was harder than I imagined, and I could not have done it without some special people in my life as well as leaders who I don't know but who make a positive impact in the lives of our future leaders.

First, I would like to thank God, Who is head of my life and through Him all things are possible.

Second is my wonderful husband, Vernon (Vito), who is my rock and love of my life. Thank you, Dear, for your support, not just working on this book but throughout our twenty-three years of marriage. You have always told me you are my biggest supporter, and you've proven that over and over again. Thank you for believing in me! I love you.

To my entire family, especially my sisters Geraldine and Ramona. Your endearing, everlasting love and prayers keep me encouraged. Thank you.

To Melissa, my best friend forever, words cannot explain my sincere appreciation for your friendship over the past forty years. As Gayle is to Oprah, so are you to me. Thank you for love and support.

Great leadership is important now more than ever. It was great leaders that inspired me to write this book. I would like to thank every great leader, present and past, for your contributions to making good leaders great. What I have learned in life is that there is a good chance that you will never know the positive impact you've made in someone's life. Great leaders are not concerned with receiving accolades or praise. Their goal is to make the world a better place for others. I have had some great leaders in my career.

One of those leaders is Coach Dick Vermeil former NFL Head Coach. I would like to thank Coach for his authentic leadership in caring not only for his players and coaches but everyone in the organization. Thank you, Coach, for making me feel appreciated and valued.

Another great leader in my life is Maxine Clark, Founder of Build-A-Bear Workshop. Maxine exemplifies a great leader who lives her life helping others reach their fullest potential. I have never seen anyone as dedicated to empowering women as Maxine. Thank you, Maxine, for believing in me and supporting me during my career as a nonprofit CEO. I will cherish the red pencil you gave me and the story behind it.

To my book contributors, Marilyn Bush, Penny Pennington, and Michelle Tucker. Words cannot express my sincere gratitude for your support. When I called, you answered and for that I say thank you. I know the readers will get valuable nuggets from your writing.

It took a village to write this book. There are so many people I want to thank but unfortunately, I cannot list them all. Those whose names are not listed, you know who you are and how much you mean to me, so thank you for your support and friendship.

I would like to start by thanking the entire Davis Creative Publishing Partners led by Cathy and Jack Davis. I would not have known where to start without your guidance, thank you.

To my patient editor, Kay Clark-Uhles. Kay, you made this daunting process fun and exciting, and I could not have done it without you. Thank you.

To my many tribes starting with my high school girlfriends, now known as Sisters4ever: Eileen, LaEatrice, Stephanie, Tera, Terri, Trish and two additions, Janette and Lece. You played a major role in who I am today. You accepted me into your tribe when I was only fourteen years old. You inspired me then and still do today. Thank you for your friendship for over forty-seven years. Love y'all.

To my AKA line sisters Alpha Delta Chapter. As I write this today, August 29, 2021, I will forever remember our weekend together celebrating forty years as line sisters. Love y'all.

To my SistersInChrist, from Shalom Church (City of Peace), Florissant, Missouri. Thank you for your continued prayers and love.

To my pastor, Rev. Dr. F. James Clark and Sister Clark, thank you for being my pastor for over twenty years. Love you both.

To my Link Sisters, Snap, Snap, thank you for your love, support, and friendship.

To my Brio Girls, it's been a joy traveling the world with you from the Baltic Seas to Greece. Thank you, ladies, for your support throughout my nonprofit career and even before.

To my Rooted Sisters, being a part of this awesome Bible study group has been my strength through some difficult times. Thank you for your love and prayers.

To my Pineapple Sisters, I am so grateful for your friendship, prayers, and support. It's wonderful sharing special moments with you ladies. What happens in Jamaica, stays in Jamaica.

To *all* my friends, whom I refuse to name for fear I'll be in trouble by leaving someone off the list, thank you for always encouraging me and taking my calls whenever I needed prayer or to celebrate a milestone in my life. You are all very special to me and I love you.

Last but not least, my executive coach, Edie Varley. Edie, words cannot express my sincere gratitude for your encouragement in writing this book. I would not have written it without your support. I wanted to give up so many times, but you held my hand each step of the way and said giving up was not option. I cannot thank you for taking time to read each chapter upon completion and giving me your honest feedback. I'll always remember your words, "You've Got this." You were right. Because of God's faithfulness, I got this! Thank you for believing in me.

Introduction

We're all interested in winning—whether at a game of chess, on a basketball court or football field, or in business. Winning teams have a lot in common with winning companies. Business, too, is a competitive sport. Clearly, it's not just up to one quarterback or one receiver or one manager or the CEO; it's up to a lot of people playing their role, blocking and tackling, supervising and motivating.

People think sports are only for men. But sports are for women too. The same is true in business. I've operated for a long time in a man's world. So did Adrian in the NFL. What Adrian brings to the table is that feminine business mindset. As a leader in the NFL, Adrian dealt with men who had incredible talent and great strength, physically and mentally, who made millions of dollars. She stood shoulder-to-shoulder with owners and managers. She approached problems as a woman. She didn't try to be a man, couldn't be a player. That wasn't her deal. But she was able to have a huge impact and she's able to bring that learning of a football player to a non-football-player environment—an environment that helps growing people use those same skills. As CEO, she was able to apply these principles in rebuilding YWCA Metro St. Louis where she helped women go from poverty to prosperity.

Historically, women have been underestimated in sports and business environments. Prejudice starts first by being a woman. But women who come from different backgrounds, different ethnicities, are needed in leadership positions in a man's world. Managing a company or a nonprofit organization is a team sport. Adrian has seen it all and she applies her business skills to doing better for people, helping people aspire to places they might not go by themselves. Having had experience in the sports industry, Adrian brings extra skills necessary to compete in the business world. She brings this unique perspective to leadership and shares that perspective in *Halftime: Learn to Pivot as a Leader and Identify Your Next Step.*

Winning takes a team. We know that players with a winning mindset and personal accountability build winning and successful teams, on the field or in business; they enjoy their work so they come back, they come to work, healthy, happy. Teams need talent and talent has value in return on investment. I mean revenue is the word. Might be revenue for a for-profit business or nonprofit. You need people who can bring in the resources that you need to provide the services that you intend to deliver.

Winning takes a plan. A game plan, like a business plan, helps teams to execute. Adrian followed her game plan as she accomplished each goal and achieved her ultimate purpose. Providing that game plan or that business plan, which might be for only you to see, is a critical part of convincing yourself that you can do this, that you should do this, and that other people need you to do this.

Adrian brings multiple careers to the table to do what all business people do to solve problems. Business needs women—women from all walks of life—for the unique perspective they bring to the boardroom. Women in general have been underestimated for their potential to contribute. Women leaders have the same brains that are necessary to run a play. Adrian has a perspective that is incredibly valuable. As you read *Halftime: Learn to Pivot as a Leader and Identify Your Next Step*, you'll be saying "She's more like me than I thought, and I can learn from her experience."

Maxine Clark
Founder, Build-A-Bear Workshop

Chapter One:

My Half-Time Story

Don't give up at halftime.
Concentrate on winning the second half.

—Paul (Bear) Bryant, late college football player and coach

In football, teams take advantage of halftime to reflect and make adjustments, if necessary. Halftime provides an opportunity to pivot and learn from what worked and what did not during the first half. The same is true in business and our personal lives. Halftime allows us to pivot and make necessary adjustments to achieve our goals. Every now and then, whether in our careers or our lives, we should stop and take inventory of the direction of our journeys. In my life, I have had several pivoting moments. I call them my "halftimes" and have welcomed each of them as a time to stop and reflect, to make critical changes to either prevent or overcome losses. At the time of this book, I'm sixty years old and excited about my second half (and sixty is the new forty!)

These are my half-time stories and lessons learned...

I grew up in Miami, Florida, in a neighborhood called "Liberty City." The youngest of six children, I knew something was different when I was about four years old because I did not live in the same house as my siblings. When I turned six years old, I understood that my biological mother was ill and not able to take care of me. After my birth, she took me to my paternal grand-aunt and uncle's home to live with them and their family. She left me in a shoe box on the step where my grand-aunt found me.

Mental illness is something that society and families are ashamed of and do not want to discuss. If society addressed this illness in the open, more lives would be saved today. Unfortunately, my mother suffered from mental illness, but even still, she wanted the best for me as a baby and took me to my grand-aunt's home where she knew they would take care of me.

Life was up and down growing up. When I was eight years old, a family member told me that I was dumb and would end up like my mother: in the mental hospital. I believed it and made poor grades in elementary school. Then at age ten, I was adopted by my cousins, Dorothy and Joel Brown.

My adoptive parents built the foundation for my faith and taught me how to pray, believe, and trust in God. Dorothy reminded me that, from Psalm 139:14, I was "fearfully and wonderfully made." Dorothy, my new mom, known as "Mom Dot," told me that I was smart and could be anybody I wanted to be if I studied hard and made good grades. My grades took a drastic turn for the better. I became an A/B student throughout high school all because Mom Dot told me that I was smart, and I believed her.

The power of positive thinking is real. I learned it at an early age, not knowing what it even meant. Now I realize that was my first half-time experience. I made an adjustment that changed the trajectory of my life, all because I prayed, received, and activated my faith in God.

When I entered high school in the ninth grade, I noticed six young ladies that I thought were smart and beautiful. I invited myself to join their clique. Today, we are still good friends. I call them, “Spa Divas”: Terri, Tera, LaEatrice, Trish, Eileen, and Stephanie. My high school spa divas encouraged me to run for Miss Miami Edison High. They campaigned for me, and I won the title in my senior year. Today, we have two additional divas, Janette and Lece. We take spa getaways together bi-annually and sometimes in between when possible. I am proud of my sisters. We now call ourselves “Sisters4Ever.” Maybe you’ve heard the statement, “Iron sharpens iron.” That statement is true for me. My Sisters4Ever are my iron; they’ve made me sharper than I would be without them. From my spa divas, I learned the importance of surrounding myself with people who make more deposits than withdrawals in my life. With the encouragement of Mom Dot and my spa divas, I made it to college—we all made it college and became individually successful in our own right.

My advice to you, my readers, is to surround yourself with people who want the same thing you want out of life, people who will encourage you to be the best you can be and not settle for less. Deciding to become friends with these six ladies, my Sisters4ever, instead of the kids in my neighborhood was a half-time moment, a pivot in my life that I will never regret.

During a college visitation day with my high school counselor and other students, I encountered my first experience of racism. At the Florida college we were visiting, a white guy yelled down from his second-floor dorm, “Go Home [N-word].”

After that experience, I decided to attend a Historically Black College/University (HBCU) so I could get the nurturing that I needed. That was another half-time moment. You see, in my senior year of high school, my counselor encouraged me to attend a majority university instead of a minority university. She said that I would have a better chance of having a successful career. I was torn at the time, but I followed my heart and I chose Morgan State University in Baltimore, Maryland. Besides, I had family in Baltimore.

My aunt, Sophronia, and my cousin, Vicki, welcomed me into their home and life in Baltimore. When I entered Morgan, I wanted to major in law, but my college counselor suggested I try accounting based on my SAT score and high school transcripts. I took one accounting course and never looked back. It is important to take advice from those with experience. Because of my college counselor's advice, I met an accounting student, Helen, who, still today, is one of my best of friends. I also met Melissa at Morgan, and today after forty years, she is still my BFF.

Because of my experiences, my major in accounting, and the people I met, I had a great college life at Morgan State.

After graduating from college and living in Baltimore for several more years, I wanted to return to my hometown, Miami, Florida, to be near my family—but I was afraid. I had a great life in Baltimore and loved Maryland-style crab cakes, as well as blue crabs! I loved wearing my winter clothes and Baltimore's four seasons. I loved being close to New York and Washington, DC. For a twenty-something-year-old young lady, I had a good life. However, I found myself at halftime and needing to make a decision. Am I ready to adjust and change my lifestyle, or do

I remain in Baltimore where I am comfortable and feel safe in my career?

In football, sometimes a coach will have to call a risky play to try and win the game. It may not feel comfortable, but he will never know if it will work unless he tries. If he is successful, he is a genius; if he fails, well, you know what people will call him: "stupid."

My profession as an accountant made me conservative and less likely to take risks. However, when I looked back on my life and realized I had taken a risk by leaving Miami to attend college in Baltimore, I was less fearful to move back home to Miami.

Again, in football, each team prepares its strategy to win the game. The coaching staff develops a strategy which is called the "game plan." Without a game plan we are doomed to fail. I think of the game plan as a roadmap. I remember growing up in Miami and hearing news reports about tourists who would not use a road map after renting a car. Instead, they would get lost in a bad neighborhood and end up being robbed—or worse, killed—all because they did not have a clear direction toward their destination.

If you don't know where you are going,
you'll end up someplace else.

—Yogi Berra, late baseball player

Many of us work in companies where a strategic plan is considered the bible of the company, yet many of us do not have a strategic plan for ourselves. We live year after year with a feeling that there is something else out there for us to do, but we just do not know what it is. Well, having a game plan for life is a start.

When I returned to Miami, I found a great job in an aviation company and was quite happy for most of five years. However, management changed, and the new president wanted a man in my position. Well, instead of hiring a man for my position, he created a new position—that is, chief of staff. After his hire, instead of reporting to the president, I started reporting to the new chief of staff. I was livid! I came to another halftime in my life. I needed to decide whether to make a change or remain on a job where I was miserable. I found the courage to leave. I found a new job in a manufacturing company where I was happy for eight months.

Then I received a call from a colleague, and that began my eighteen-year career in the National Football League (NFL).

When I meet someone, the first question I always get is, "How did you get a job in the NFL?" I tell the story of the importance of networking and being a part of a professional organization. Networking opens up opportunities to meet like-minded people. I mean, you never know who you will meet in a professional organization. I know men and women who have met their spouses in these organizations.

When I moved back to Miami, I joined a professional organization called "National Association of Black Accountants" (NABA). As a member of NABA, I volunteered to be the director of student affairs. In that role, I tutored college students who majored in accounting. I took the work very seriously—as though it was a paid position. I knew firsthand how difficult accounting was and had been fortunate enough to be tutored during my college years. I wanted to pay it forward.

One day I received an invitation to lunch from a friend and colleague in NABA. He said, confidentially, "I have interviewed for the controller's position for the Miami Dolphins, and I used"—let's call him—"'George' as a reference."

I knew George but he was not a close friend. However, when I returned to my office after having lunch with my NABA colleague, I received a call from George. He informed me that he had received a call from the Miami Dolphins, and he gave my name to the treasurer as a possible candidate for the controller's position. Yes, that is what I said. The same position for which my friend and colleague had also interviewed.

I interviewed with the executives of the Miami Dolphins and Joe Robbie Stadium. I was hired. Afterwards, I called my NABA friend, to tell him that I was hired as the controller for the Miami Dolphins. Needless to say, we are no longer friends.

The lesson learned is to do your absolute best in whatever task you undertake. George, also a member of NABA but whom I had not known well, referred me to the Miami Dolphins based on my hard work as director of student affairs for NABA, a volunteer position. As you can see, it is not always who you know but who knows you. Always do your best and you will be noticed and rewarded. But even if you are not noticed or rewarded, be proud of yourself and celebrate your success!

When I was growing up in Miami, the only professional sports team was the Miami Dolphins. So I have this great job working for the Miami Dolphins, my hometown team. As you can imagine, I was working a dream job, right? It was a dream job, however, I found myself at halftime, again, after a year or so. I was bored. I had just left a high-energy job as a controller for a manufacturing company, a blue-collar industry. I had used all my education in that job: cost accounting, tax accounting, auditing, et cetera. I had traded that job for work with a prestigious NFL team, which I considered an easy and low-stress job compared to my former employment. I shared my boredom with a few family members and friends. Everyone encouraged me to find a way to add excitement to my job. I tried things like setting up a new general ledger and creating budgets, but nothing seemed to work. I know that doesn't sound exciting for most people, but for an accountant, it can be exciting.

There I was again at halftime. I needed to make a decision on my career. Do I stay with the NFL because of the prestige, or do I look for something more interesting? I know what you are thinking to yourself: "What could be more interesting than working for an NFL team?"

Regardless of my boredom, I decided to stay with the Miami Dolphins. I made the best of it for four more years; then after much prayer, I decided it was time to leave the Dolphins, another half-time decision.

In 1995, I heard about the Los Angeles Rams moving to St. Louis. I used my networking skills and made contact with a colleague, my former boss with Joe Robbie Stadium, who then was working in New York for the NFL. He made the connection for me with the then-president of the St. Louis Rams, John Shaw.

I first visited St. Louis for my interview as vice president of finance for the St. Louis Rams. I remember flying over St. Louis thinking how dull it appeared compared to Miami. I saw brown patches from the sky and thought, *Am I ready to live in farmland*? I stayed in St. Louis over the weekend to get a feel. To my surprise, St. Louis was a nice town—a small town with a big-city feel. After I was offered the position with the St. Louis Rams, I told a colleague who then lived in Miami, but was born in St. Louis, that I would be moving to St. Louis. He could not believe I was leaving the Miami Dolphins to work for the St. Louis Rams. He called the Rams the "Lambs," as so many others did. He said to me, "Why would you leave a Mercedes Benz to work for a Pinto?" Some of my readers may not know what a Pinto (the car) looks like since it no longer exists. In the 1990's, the Pinto was a very inexpensive car or, as some would say, a "cheap" car, with a bad reputation.

While making my decision to leave Miami, the Dolphins were a winning team, an elite franchise, and the Rams were a losing team and an underrated franchise with one of the worst records in the NFL. In the nineties, Miami was becoming a popular city for movie and music productions. The then-popular South Beach was known around the country as the new hotspot for nightlife entertainment. Tourism was growing and Miami finally had a baseball team, the Florida Marlins. Life was good for a single thirty-something young woman working for the Miami Dolphins. However, after much prayer and soul-searching, I knew it was time to move on and give St. Louis and the Rams a go.

Even though this was a risky move, I felt at peace. I did not understand it then, but now I know God was leading me to my ultimate purpose in life: inspiring and enhancing the lives of women and girls.

During my prayer time, I visualized my life in St. Louis. I saw a megachurch in my vision and a husband. To be honest, I was not interested in either. I loved my small intimate church in Miami, and I loved being single. The thought of joining a megachurch or becoming a wife was not at all appealing to me. However, I could feel deep down inside that St. Louis would become my reality.

In 1995, I started my new life in St. Louis as vice president of finance for the then-St. Louis Rams. I moved in the winter, so I was excited to be able to wear the winter clothes I had loved in Baltimore and to enjoy the four seasons once again. What I was not prepared for was driving in snow. I had forgotten about my days living in Baltimore being terrified to drive in the slick stuff.

In December of 1995, after only two months living in St. Louis, I was driving on Highway 40 headed to work in downtown St. Louis. I hit what is called "black ice" and spun around 360 degrees on the highway. By the grace of God, I did not hit anyone, nor was I injured. A friendly gentleman pulled over to help me. He explained to me what had happened and that I needed to get new tires right away. He escorted me off the highway to the nearest automotive store. He must have been an angel because I never saw the man again. That was my first experience of the wonderful hospitality I received in St. Louis. To this day, it still exists and for that, I am grateful.

After a year working for the St. Louis Rams—here I go again. I became bored with my job. I felt like it was halftime again, time for me to pivot or make an adjustment in my career. I began to wonder if I had made the wrong decision leaving the Miami Dolphins. Doubt is a very powerful force.

I knew I had to deal with my emotions. I looked inwardly, outwardly, and studied them. I learned that emotions are biological states of the nervous system brought on by neurophysiological changes associated with thoughts, feelings, behavioral responses, and the degree of pleasure or displeasure. My displeasure was boredom.

During my halftime, I once again began to pray to God for direction. After prayer, I stayed with the Rams for a while longer.

I got involved with the local chapter of NABA and other organizations in St. Louis, i.e., the National Black MBA Association (NBMBAA). It was through the NBMBAA that I met a wonderful friend, Connie. Connie was from Cleveland. Like me, she was looking to make new friends in St. Louis. Connie and I hit it off right away.

St. Louis began to grow on me; I began to love the town. And I still had the vision that Mr. Right was somewhere in St. Louis waiting to find me.

The Bible says in Proverbs 18:22, "He who finds a wife finds what is good" (NIV); it does not say a woman who finds a husband finds what is good. Just thought I would share.

In January 1997, I went to a fundraiser to represent the St. Louis Rams. I was there to present a check to the United Negro College Fund on behalf of the team. While sitting in my car outside of the venue, I felt Mr. Right would be waiting for me inside. It was a strong overwhelming feeling, so I began to pray, as I do when I need direction from God. I spoke to God like a friend and said, "Okay, God, you know I have made some bad decisions regarding men before. I feel strongly that my husband is inside this venue, so please help me not to make the same mistakes I have made in the past."

I felt a peace and calm come over me and walked inside the venue with confidence. Mr. Right greeted me at the door with a big smile. However, he was not alone. His friend, who we'll call "Edward," had accompanied him. It was Edward who made the first move on me. I did not feel right about it all, but I went along with it. Edward invited me out on a date. I accepted his invitation still not feeling comfortable about the whole thing. Edward shared with me that my Mr. Right was dating his friend, who we'll call "Pamela," and that maybe we should double date one day. I said I did not think that would be a good idea. I could not bear seeing my Mr. Right with another woman.

After two dates with Edward, I told him I was no longer interested in going out with him. A month later, Mr. Right called me and invited me to lunch. I told him that Edward had informed me he was involved in a relationship with Edward's friend Pamela. Mr. Right denied that it was a relationship but only a friendship. I told Mr. Right that I was not interested in any type of shenanigans. Three months later, Mr. Right called me to let me know he was no longer in a friendship with Pamela and he would like to take me out on a date. I accepted. A year later, my Mr. Right, Vernon "Vito" Bracy, and I were married. As of the date of this book, it has been over twenty-three years and our marriage continues to grow strong! I am a proud stepmom of Donovan, who is now twenty-eight years old.

Once I met Mr. Right, the one thing still missing from my life in St. Louis was a church to call home. Remember, I had envisioned I was a member of a megachurch in St. Louis. My new girlfriend, Connie, whom I had become very close to, introduced me to Shalom Church (City of Peace). My husband and I joined Shalom Church where we currently attend and are active members.

In 2005, after a decade as vice president of finance for the St. Louis Rams, I found myself having another half-time moment. I thought, *Is it time to make an adjustment? Is it time to pivot my career?*

Since 1999, after enjoying my first experience at a five-star spa, I longed to have my own day spa. I remember like it was yesterday. I had gone to my colleague, Allison's office to ask her opinion about leaving the NFL. She had also been contemplating making a move, so I felt comfortable speaking in confidence with her. She encouraged me to go after my dream of starting my own day-spa. It all sounded good, and I was motivated to move forward until I allowed fear to stop me. I did not follow my dreams. Instead, I stayed with the St. Louis Rams. That is, until 2007 when I learned that a colleague, who was the CFO for the Arizona Cardinals Football team in Phoenix, was retiring.

I spoke with my husband about the opportunity and he encouraged me to go for it. I sent my résumé to the president of the Arizona Cardinals, interviewed, and was offered the job. But I wasn't sure if I should take it. I was at a half-time moment once again. Is it time to pivot, make an adjustment, or stay where I am comfortable, love what I do, and have a cushy life with the Rams? Once again, after prayer, I accepted the position; Vito and I made a decision to leave St. Louis and move to Phoenix.

It was June 2007, and we had just landed in Phoenix. I knew immediately it was a mistake. You know why? It was 110 degrees!! I do not like the heat. And I had known the heat would be an issue going into the decision to move to Phoenix, but I thought I could overcome it. The problem was my husband loved Phoenix and asked if I would at least give it a chance, so I did.

Two years later, I was at halftime once again. I was not happy in Phoenix and missed St. Louis. I told my husband of my dilemma and he encouraged me to follow my heart. I had to make yet another decision, but this time it was two years into the job rather than several years. During that halftime, I prayed and asked God for direction. It was clear as day to me: Time to retire from the NFL, after nearly eighteen years, and follow my passion—inspiring and enhancing the lives of women and girls.

In May 2009, I received a call from a friend and board member of YWCA Metro St. Louis, Toni. Toni had visited Phoenix the previous year, and we had a chance to spend time together, so she knew my husband, Vito, and I were ready to relocate back to St. Louis. Toni told me about a position with the YWCA. In June that year, I interviewed for the CEO position of YWCA Metro St. Louis. I was offered the position, and my husband and I moved back to St. Louis to take on my new role in a nonprofit organization.

The mission of YWCA is "eliminating racism and empowering women." WOW! Their mission fit me perfectly. And I get paid to live out my passion and purpose in life—to inspire and enhance the lives of women and girls. To God be the glory!

Chapter Two:
Procrastination – Stop Procrastinating!

Don't wait. The time will never be just right.

—Napoleon Hill, *Think and Grow Rich*

This quote resonates with me. I have struggled with procrastination in recent years. As a teenager, I did not have a problem with procrastination because I was anxious to become a successful businesswoman. I was motivated to get things done on or before the due date. I had clearly defined goals and knew there would be future rewards if I accomplished them. One definition of procrastination, according to an article on Indeed.com, titled "11 Winning Strategies for Overcoming Procrastination" (n.d.), is that instead of completing the task at hand, you delay it for another time. An article written by Kate Meads on LinkedIn (2020) defines it as avoiding a task that needs to be completed by a certain date.

When I procrastinated, I would justify it as a good thing. I told myself and others that I worked better under pressure, so waiting until the last minute was a positive characteristic. And there was some truth to that. In college, I produced some good term papers in a matter of hours. And as a young adult in the workforce, it felt normal waiting until the last minute to turn in an assignment to my boss. However, there is a price to pay for procrastination and I have paid a big price over the years.

Most of us have procrastinated at one point or another in our lives. Like most, I have always had good reasons as to why I waited to either start or complete a task. Causes for procrastination, I believe, are based on fear, doubt, perfectionism, boredom, and distractions—albeit good distractions, but distractions, nonetheless. And I mean distractions, like spending too much time talking on the telephone or watching television, text messaging, social-media surfing, et cetera. I also believe lack of clarity, direction, or time cause us to procrastinate; as well as lack of self-confidence and motivation; lack of self-control or discipline. We put things off for many reasons, but these are some of the most common. And I have experienced all of them at some point in my life. Fear and doubt are the biggest for me.

Fear is an unpleasant emotion caused by the belief that someone or something is dangerous, likely to cause pain or a threat to our safety. I have seen an acronym of fear: "False Expectations Appearing Real." I used to believe that, but I have learned that fear is not always false expectations appearing real. Fear can be real and should be taken into consideration before making major decisions. Fear can be our friend. If we feel very strongly about something and our gut tells us to beware, we should pay attention. Sometimes it is God's way of telling us we are on the wrong path. It's like GPS, "God's Positioning System," keeping us from making the wrong turn.

While fear can be our friend, it can also be our detractor. Fear can hold us back from achieving our dreams. We may suffer from the fear of what people will think about us if we fail; the fear of not having enough money to fulfill our dream; the fear of success. I know the fear of success may sound ridiculous. After all, many people dream of success, but some people may also fear success. And remember, success is personal. What success means to one person may not mean the same for someone else. We may look for success in business or in our personal lives. For purposes of this book, though, I refer to success as it pertains to one's career.

I grew up in humble beginnings, not really knowing what a successful businesswoman looked like; I just knew that was my dream. My biological father taught school; my adoptive father drove a bus. Neither my biological mother nor my adoptive mother graduated with a college degree. But a college degree does not signify wisdom. The one thing my adoptive mother, Dorothy, taught me was to trust God.

At age fourteen when I entered high school in the ninth grade, I wasn't able to articulate the meaning of a successful career, primarily because I had no role model to demonstrate what a successful career looked like. What I had was a loving family who wanted the best for my life. Mom Dot told me that if I worked hard in school and received good grades, I could go to college and become a successful businesswoman or whatever I wanted to be. That alone scared me because it meant I would be the first sibling in my family to graduate from college. I guess I should have been excited, but it felt like a lot of pressure at the time.

As I said before, when I was eight years old, a cousin told me I was dumb and stupid, and that I would end up in a mental ward like my biological mom. I believed that until I was adopted. So the thought of me going to college was scary. I was afraid that I was not smart enough, rich enough, or pretty enough. To add to those fears, I was an eight-year-old black girl who believed the stereotypical comments, such as that black kids were inferior to white kids. Fortunate for me, God sent Mom Dot to tell me different and I believed her. I am sure that my biological mother, Elizabeth, would have agreed with Mom Dot, but she was not there to influence me. Because of Mom Dot's new message of encouragement, I began to study hard and graduated from high school with honors. I also graduated from college with honors and a bachelor's degree in accounting.

As an adult, I learned the first step of overcoming fear was having self-awareness that fear existed. Once I accepted that fact, I had to be willing to name the fear. Then I became curious about why I was afraid. Once I accepted that I was afraid, identified the fear, and discovered why I was afraid, then I was able to deal with and find solutions to overcome my fear. One solution for me: I hired a counselor. Having someone to talk to about my fear benefitted me and my career. Yes, it was uncomfortable at times but necessary for me to peel back the layers to see and understand the root cause of my fear. Experience is the best teacher, so by practicing through my own experiences, I learned how to overcome fear with faith.

To me, doubt is the opposite of faith. It's when I'm not sure something will materialize or come to fruition. I certainly have had doubt throughout my career, and doubt has hindered me from pursuing my dream. Like I mentioned before, I visited my first spa in 1999 while working for the St. Louis Rams. I had attended the NFL's annual March owner's meeting. After the meetings were over, I decided, while the guys played golf, I would go to the five-star day spa at the resort. It did not disappoint. I felt relaxed and balanced.

After that day, I felt my life's destiny bubble up from deep down inside me; that destiny was to own a day spa. I have dreamed about it ever since. I wanted every girlfriend, and even women I did not know, to experience the same relaxation and balance I had. After that, I developed my personal mission statement: "to inspire and enhance the lives of women and girls." I envisioned that each client's experience in my own day spa would do just that. I was sincere about pursuing my dream.

The first thing I did was get support and blessings from my husband. He gave it fully. He said, "I am in it to win it and I have your back." I created a strategic plan for my dream. I scheduled meetings with current spa owners to learn about their failures and successes. I met with a real estate agent to locate the perfect place for my day spa. And we found it! It sat close to the highway but was secluded enough to offer the spa ambience. I then met with my financing bank to seal the deal. All of the pieces were coming together. It felt like my dream was finally coming to fruition. Then I found myself at another half-time life experience. I needed to make a decision whether to stay working in the NFL or step out on faith and start my own day spa. As any CPA would do, I started to analyze everything from A to Z.

I shared my dream with people—the wrong people. Big mistake! Some of my family and friends told me I would be crazy to give up such a prestigious career in the NFL to start

a business that was not guaranteed to succeed. I allowed doubt to settle into my mind. Along with fear, it consumed my thoughts. I found myself procrastinating on tasks that needed to get done. My husband began to question the sincerity of my commitment to own my own day spa. I found myself making excuses of why I should wait until next year.
Year after year passed and still nothing. "Next year" never came.

Fear and doubt together act as a powerful duo, and I let them both into my halftime decision to open a day spa. Together, they were a formidable force capable of pushing me away from my passion and purpose of inspiring and enhancing the lives of women and girls.

In the past, I have experienced fear without doubt and proceeded to achieve a goal. I feared that I could not stay focused, but I had no doubt that my goal could be accomplished. I also have experienced doubt without fear. I had doubt that I would actually complete a six-mile run, but fear did not enter my mind and I achieved my goal. But being afraid and doubtful, both, when facing one goal is a whole different story.

So with fear and doubt's interjection, I took the safe and secure way of life. I decided to stay with the NFL and forego my dream. After all, I had a good pension plan, health insurance, a good salary, paid vacation, and a prestigious career in the NFL. I was afraid to let go of the comfortable and predictable lifestyle of working in the NFL and had doubts that I even wanted to run my own day spa.

Now, you may notice that I did not mention asking God for direction in owning my own day spa. In fact, I did not ask God then or to this day. The reason I did not is because—and this is where my self-awareness and naming my fear came in—I was afraid that if I asked God to remove my fear and doubt, He would do it and I would be accountable to move forward with starting my day spa. The truth is, I was afraid not that I would fail but that I would succeed. We typically talk about the fear of failure, but I actually had the fear of success. I feared the spa becoming a huge success. I feared not being ready for, one, attention, and two, ownership. Let's unpack what I mean.

We talk a lot about being our authentic selves. My innate nature is that of an introvert. I know it is hard for people to believe that about me because they see me as outgoing. The truth is I would rather be by myself reading a book than at a celebrity party. My current role requires me to perform as an extrovert, so I've learned to adjust. For my career, I've had to pivot to fit in. And it paid off. Being flexible helped me to enhance my leadership skills.

Back to the discussion at hand. What was I afraid of? I believed that if the spa became successful, people would expect more from me—like my time, talents, and treasures. I am a giving person, so the treasures I had no problem with; but the mere thought of giving up my time and talents scared me. I envisioned the spa being so successful that I would actually be on the *Oprah Winfrey Show*. That thought terrified me to death. I was not interested in that type of success, so I talked myself out of my dream. In addition, truth be told, I was not willing to work that hard.

Throughout this entire ordeal, as always, my husband stayed by my side and supported my decision to stay with the St. Louis Rams football team.

So, again, in 2007, while still working for the Rams, I got the itch. Previously, I had decided not to pursue my dream of owning my own day spa, but I still wanted a change. What I did not have at that moment was clear direction of what I wanted to do next. So I felt as though I was in another half-time moment. What adjustments did I need to make? Was there a pivoting opportunity or should I stay with the Rams and reconstruct my job description to give me the feel of a new job?

Halftimes give us a chance to dream big. To imagine our BHAG (Big Hairy Audacious Goals). I love that about halftimes!

Way back in 2004, I had written down some goals. One goal I set was staying in the NFL. But during my halftime in 2007, I wasn't sure what direction to take anymore. So I did what I usually do when I need direction (except when deciding about my day spa): I prayed and asked God for direction.

During my career, getting and keeping a job in the NFL was not an easy task. I assume it's the same today. In general, CFOs in the NFL either get sick and leave, get fired, die, or retire. So after I prayed for direction, I left it alone and went on my merry way. That's when my colleague informed me about the CFO position with the Arizona Cardinals. I applied for the job and got it. My first thought was *This must be God directing me to my destiny*.

Phoenix, Arizona, is one of the best spa destinations in America. And even though I had put my dream of opening a day spa into the "no" column on my overall game plan, it still predominated my thoughts. So I assumed that working for the Cardinals would be a steppingstone to opening my own day spa. For the two years we lived in Phoenix, I visited every four- or five-star-rated day spa in the area. I enjoyed the experiences with no regrets. However, I was at halftime again. *Do I stay with the NFL or do I leave to start my own day spa?* Like before, I had no clear direction or focus as to my next journey. The lack of clarity and direction can stop any journey toward success. My husband and I discussed leaving Phoenix; I paused to ask God for clarity. Clarity came. This was not my time to start a day spa, but instead it was a time to make a major decision in my life.

In May 2008, when my good friend and board member of YWCA Metro St. Louis, Toni, came to Phoenix on vacation, she asked how I was doing. This is when I told her the truth. I was not happy and really missed St. Louis.

She said, "We will get you back to St. Louis."

I believed her. I did not know what it meant, but I believed her and wanted to be prepared for my next journey.

In October 2008, I attended a Stephen Covey's webinar entitled "Writing Your Personal Mission Statement." And I did just that; I wrote my personal mission statement—"to inspire and enhance the lives of women and girls"—during that webinar. I was clear about my mission but not clear about what to do with it.

So while working for the Arizona Cardinals, finding myself at halftime, and needing to make a decision on my career, again, I had doubt about my future. *What was I going to do if I left the NFL?* But after taking the Covey webinar on my personal mission statement, I got clear on my vision. I felt whatever direction I took would include helping women and girls. I had no idea it would be in nonprofit. If we get clear about our vision, it will help us get clear about what priorities we need to take to achieve our vision.

I have had a passion for helping women and girls my entire life. I fulfilled that passion certainly not by working for the NFL, but by sitting on the board of directors for Girls, Inc. of St. Louis and YWCA Metro St. Louis while working for the St. Louis Rams

After two years with the Arizona Cardinals and not having fulfilled my passion, I was looking for change. In May 2009, Toni—in keeping with her promise to get me back to St. Louis—called me with the news that the CEO of YWCA Metro St. Louis was retiring and asked me to send her my résumé. I doubted that I could run a nonprofit; after all, I had been an accountant my entire career. But I sent her my résumé and received a call from the search firm. I interviewed for the position. They offered me the job, and I began my new career journey in nonprofit on August 17, 2009. That's the story of my career, transitioning from NFL to NFP (not-for-profit) and fulfilling my passion in the workplace to inspire and empower women and girls.

With my experiences in the NFL and in NFP, I realized I had something to share. I have wanted to write a book for ten years. I have paid thousands of dollars in my attempts to accomplish this goal. When I became serious about writing a book, I mustered up the nerve to do something radical—to accomplish a BHAG (big hairy audacious goal). To do something that's out of my character.

I gathered up—what I considered to be—my impressive credentials; that is, the cover of a 2003 *Black Enterprise Magazine* depicting me and several other financial professionals; a photo of me with the 1999 St. Louis Rams Greatest Show on Turf Super Bowl trophy, and other magazines I had appeared in, along with items that I thought would at least open the door for discussion of my qualifications for writing a book on leadership. I called the establishment I intended to work with to get the name of the person I should address my proposal to. I packed everything up, wrote a sincere letter about my request for support in writing a book, and went to the post office to mail my items. Because of the valuable nature (at least to me) of the items, I included a return envelope just in case the receiver was not interested in my request and my book. I addressed my letter to one of the most famous, if not *the* most famous, African-American bishops/pastors in the world, Bishop T.D. Jakes, pastor of Potter's House. I was excited and proud of myself for taking this big step.

I had decided not to tell anyone about what I had done in case it did not turn out positive. I waited two weeks after I had mailed my proposal. No response. I became anxious and thought I should call and check on the progress of my request but decided against it; I decided to have faith that God's will be done. Nearly three weeks later, I received my return envelope with all the credentials I had sent to Bishop Jakes. The envelope also included a nice rejection letter.

I was devastated and glad I had not told anyone of my adventure; otherwise, I would have been devastated and embarrassed. I felt like a failure—one of the reasons for procrastination. Before sending my request to Bishop Jakes, I had planned to send my credentials to Oprah, but after being rejected by Jakes, I lacked confidence. In hindsight, I wondered if including the return envelope was a sign of my lack of confidence; but who knows, maybe they would have rejected me without the return envelope.

After that experience, I came up with one excuse after the other of why not to write a book. I asked myself, *Who would want to read my book?* And besides, I didn't have a theme or focus on what I wanted to write. At first, I thought about a biography but realized that was boring to me, so I was sure it would be boring to others. I procrastinated longer and did nothing.

I had one excuse after the other. The biggest excuse I used was time. I never had enough time to sit down and write. So I thought if I hired a ghostwriter, I would not have to do much work. Then the ghostwriter said they needed to spend time with me so I could tell my story. Problem was, I didn't have time. Of course, the cost for a ghostwriter also deterred writing the book, so I decided not to use a ghostwriter. I procrastinated again and did absolutely nothing to pursue my dream. I allowed years to pass by just thinking about writing a book.

Several years later, I attended a women's conference with my girlfriend Connie. We both attended a workshop on the BHAG. I told Connie my BHAG was to write a book. A few weeks later, after the conference, Connie mailed me a business card of a book coach in St. Louis. I met with the book coach and decided to hire her to help me to write my book. A year later and thousands of dollars short, I had no book. It was not the book coach's fault; it was mine. I lacked motivation to write a book. I could not answer the question, "Why do you want to write a book?" I lacked the confidence that I could actually write a book that people would want to read; and, I had no discipline to schedule time in my day to sit down and write. I told myself, "I do not like to write. I'm an accountant. Just show me the numbers." Words are powerful, and I began to believe my own words…that is, I was not a writer, and the only way I would write a book is if someone else wrote it for me.

In 2020, during the pandemic, I hired an executive coach to help me with some future plans in my life. A colleague and friend, Susan, introduced me to Edie Varley. Edie is a pistol. After an hour with her, I felt motivated, energized, and ready to take on the world. I knew she was the right coach for me.

During our third session, I mentioned to Edie that one of my goals was to write a book. She asked me the question I had asked myself: "WHY? Why do you want to write a book?"

I wasn't sure how to respond to her. I remembered that in September 2019 Coach Dick Vermeil asked me the same question: "WHY?" He said, "There are enough books on leadership. What will make your book different?" I did not have an answer for Coach and changed the subject abruptly. I wanted to do the same with Edie, but something deep down inside said I could trust her and I should share my thoughts with her. So I did.

After I told Edie the title of the book, she became so intrigued that she wanted to know more. My thoughts came easily. Edie took notes. At the end of our session, she enthusiastically said, "You got it baby!"

Within an hour of that meeting, Edie emailed me her notes from our session. She had noted all ten chapters I had spoken of in our conversation. This blew me away. It was the first time someone had taken the time to actually coach me through the journey of writing a book. The thing is, Edie is not a book coach, which is even more amazing to me. I was convinced that our relationship was a God thing and not a coincidence.

As I write this book today, I am a recovering procrastinator. I've learned to be intentional in order to overcome procrastination, to rely on someone who will hold me accountable, and to talk out my goals—even in a stream of consciousness.

You don't have to see the whole staircase,
just take the first step.

—Dr. Martin Luther King, Jr.

Chapter Three:

Game Plan – Goals, Strategy, Practice, and Execution

Before you can get what you want, you have to know what you want, and make a game plan to get it.
—Jeffrey Gitomer, *The Little Red Book of Sales Answers*

"Game plan." The concept can be defined in numerous ways. My definition of game plan is having a strategy, tactic, or an approach that will help to achieve an objective, especially in sports, politics, business, and the military. In business, we typically call our game plan a "strategic plan," a thought-out strategy or course of action and a plan for achieving success. So if it is important to have a game plan in sports, politics, business, and military organizations, it is surely important to have a game plan for a career.

Without a game plan and without a strong sense of faith in what you're doing, it's going to be real hard to accomplish anything.
—Nipsey Hussle, late rapper, civil rights activist, entrepreneur

I attended a Historically Black College/University to receive the nurturing I needed as a young adult. I selected Morgan State University in Baltimore, Maryland. A month before classes, Morgan State required all incoming freshmen to attend an orientation. During orientation, my counselor suggested I take an accounting course. I told her, "Thank you for your advice, but I want to be an attorney." I had my game plan, and I was determined it was the right thing for me. She was gracious and said, "I understand, but as I look at your transcript and SAT scores, I believe you'll do great in accounting."

I confessed to her my unfamiliarity with accounting. She asked if I had heard of bookkeeping. I said yes. I had been good at bookkeeping in high school, but I wanted to be a lawyer. To appease my counselor, I signed up for a course in accounting; but I also signed up for a course in political science to prove to her that I would be good in law. After the semester, I had an "A" in accounting and I barely made a "B" in political science. I made a pivot to my new game plan. I changed my major to accounting.

Make a game plan and stick to it.
Unless it's not working.

—Yogi Berra, late baseball player

Changing my major to accounting was the best decision I could have made for my long-term career. Sure, I would have been a good attorney, but I would not have had the amazing career journey that I've had. Because I was willing to listen and take the advice of my counselor, someone experienced and knowledgeable, I graduated from college with honors and a bachelor of science degree in accounting. I went on to obtain my CPA license. My experience was instrumental not only for me but for others that I've mentored along the way.

I had known since my senior year in college that one day I wanted to be the chief financial officer (CFO) for a company. After college graduation, I didn't have a game plan, but I was very certain I did not want to work in public accounting. I kept my eye on being a CFO. I spoke with career accountants who told me that, unless I worked in public accounting, I would never make it as CFO. Meaning, I needed to work for a firm that employed accountants who served businesses, individuals, nonprofits, and governmental organizations before venturing into my dream job as a CFO.

In 1982 when I graduated from college, eight major professional public accounting firms, known as the "Big 8," existed. Friends and colleagues told me that, if I did not work for a Big 8 accounting firm, my chances of becoming a CFO one day were slim to none. But I did not want to work for a public accounting firm. During those days, Big 8 firms were not an easy place to work for African Americans; they did not feel supported—or welcomed for that matter. Most of my colleagues who took positions in one of the Big 8 only lasted a year or two due to prejudice and discrimination. In addition, they were given assignments no one else wanted. It was primarily for these reasons that the National Association of Black Accountants was created; that is, to support and encourage African-American accountants, to offer the opportunity to share experiences, and to network in a safe space.

So after college, I decided I would take my chances and work for a private or public corporation where I could learn the business and grow with the company. I was not naïve in believing there would be no discrimination in corporate America, but I knew myself and knew my personality would make a better fit working in a corporation rather than in public accounting.

My career story started in 1982. A dear friend, Kim Griffin Hunter, started her career in 1988, six years after me. She decided to take the path of public accounting and took a position as a public accountant for Deloitte. Remember, in 1982, the Big 8 public accounting firms cornered much of the public accounting market. Deloitte Haskins & Sells was one of them. Today, in 2020, only four firms remain and are now known as the "Big 4." I am thrilled to share with you that Kim's resilience paid off. In 1999 she became the first African-American female to be named partner ("Big 6" at the time) in the State of Florida, and in 2019 she was named the first African-American female to become managing partner for now the "Big 4" in Miami, Florida.

For those of you who are majoring in accounting or know someone who is, remember, you can achieve your dreams if you don't give up on them. Kim knew her dream and she didn't give up on it. When she first started out, I asked her what her dream was. She said to one day become a managing partner. So first, like Kim, you need to know your dreams.

I always say "to thyself be true." And to be true to myself, I continued to follow my dream to be a CFO in a corporation. Once I knew public accounting was not for me, I stayed in my lane and ran my race, not someone else's race or the race someone else wanted me to run. My race.

Determine what you want and why you want it. Once you understand what's important, you can utilize your passions and achieve anything.

—Brooke Griffin, *Skinny Suppers*

I was fortunate. I did not have to look for a job after college graduation. Throughout college, I had stuck on my game plan to work for a company; and during my junior year, I started working part-time for *The Baltimore Sun*, which is the largest general-circulation daily newspaper based in Maryland. Several months before graduation, I contacted the human resources department and asked for a meeting to share with them my game plan. They granted me the meeting, where I explained that I would be graduating in May with a bachelor's degree in accounting and would be interested in becoming full-time at the newspaper. The manager told me that if something opened up in the accounting department, they would give me a call. Less than two months later, I received a call from human resources. A newly created position would be available and waiting for me in May! To that point, my game plan was on target.

If you fail to plan, you are planning to fail.

—Benjamin Franklin

Two years later, I found myself at halftime. I loved working for *The Baltimore Sun* (the *Sun*). I had applied my education to my job and learned so much from my supervisor, but I wanted more money and was ready for a change. I needed to make a decision about my career with the *Sun*.

Halftime gives us an opportunity to evaluate our position. What's working and what's not working; then we can create a strategy to pivot or stay where we are. I listed the pros and the cons to working with the *Sun*. After much consideration and prayer, I shared my desires with a friend, Eileen. In less than a month, Eileen called me. An accounts payable manager position had become available at the ad agency she worked for. I applied for and got the job.

My new job and the people I worked with satisfied me. However, two years later, once again, I was at halftime. This time the job had not created my halftime; rather, it was my grandmother's health.

My biological father had died a week after my graduation from college. Although I had been adopted by cousins, Dorothy and Joel, my biological dad and I were close. I spent my grief in Baltimore and not in my hometown of Miami, Florida, close to my family. I felt guilt for not being in Miami when he died.

After my father died, although she never made me feel guilty, my grandmother wanted me to move back home. After all, she was getting older and needed someone to assist her with chores. Moving from Baltimore back to Miami was a difficult decision for me.

I loved living in Baltimore. I loved the seafood, especially the Maryland crab cakes. I had pledged Alpha Kappa Alpha Sorority, Incorporated at Morgan State University, and I remained close to some of my sorority sisters. I was also close to my cousin Vicki and her mom, Aunt Sophronia. Besides them, I had made other close girlfriends, like Melissa, Tomasine, and Helen. My oldest friend in the world, Darlene, had also moved to Baltimore with my goddaughter, Tawonna, to live with me. I would have to share the news with all these people that I was considering moving back home to Miami.

Leaving my first goddaughter, Tawonna, concerned me the most. She and I were close from her birth. When Tawonna and her mother moved from Miami to Baltimore to live with me, our relationship grew even closer. I was her "second mom." Our love for each other could not have been stronger had we been biologically related.

I took all of this into consideration in my decision to leave Baltimore.

During my halftime, I prayed and asked God for His direction for my life. After prayer, I knew I needed to get my game plan in place.

The first thing I had to do was send my résumé to Miami for job opportunities. A family member sent me the newspaper—yes, the newspaper by mail; we did not have Indeed.com or Google to search for a job then. I replied to several openings and received a call from one, an aviation company. I flew home to Miami for the interview. Two weeks later, they offered me the position. I felt a calm and peace, which confirmed to me that I was making the right decision.

As you can imagine, it was a tough good-bye in Baltimore and—just as I was afraid—my goddaughter took it extremely hard. I managed to get through the good-byes with painful emotions, but I made it.

In 1986, I moved back home to Miami, Florida, primarily, to be with my grandmother. Like most families, we had our disputes and arguments; but at the end of the day, everyone agreed I should move in with her. At that time, Mom Dot was my support system, and if she thought it was best, then so be it.

I started my new job in Miami at the aviation company. I was the first African-American female to be named assistant controller. After one year, the controller was terminated, and I was promoted to the controller's position. The human resources director, Eleanor, was also an African-America woman. The two of us became good friends and shared a lot of "woe-is-mes" together. She helped me recruit some great talent.

I loved my job at the aviation company and my co-workers. After five years on the job, the president of the company called me into his office to tell me he would be leaving to return to his home country, Israel. I was devasted. In my first year there, he had realized I was doing all the work while the controller took all the credit; he had seen straight through the controller and terminated him. He had promoted me to the controller's position. After that promotion, I was excited and worked even harder to prove I was worthy of the position. I wanted to make him proud of his decision to promote me, a Black woman, to controller. I would miss him.

The incoming president, also from Israel, began his new job. Right away, I knew a different management philosophy had come with him. The new president was obviously uncomfortable working with a woman—a Black woman at that. I did my best to assure the new president that I was competent, that I knew what I was doing, and that I had experience—including the experience of converting accounting systems. Twice! The previous president and I had converted a large accounting-system at the aviation company from a manual pegboard system to an updated, automated system; and I had assisted with a software conversion of the accounting system at *The Baltimore Sun*. I had confidence in what I was doing and I wanted it to show.

Unfortunately, the new president did not have the same confidence in me as the former president. He showed his doubt in my ability to run an accounting department, and it did not take him long to decide to make a change in leadership. He created a new position and hired a man to be the new chief of staff. Both the new president and new chief of staff encouraged me to remain a part of the executive team despite the new structure that was put in place, and they both developed confidence in my ability; but I no longer would report to the president—I would report to the newly created chief of staff position. My new boss was nice enough, but my pride and self-esteem would not allow me to be happy with this new structure. I found myself in halftime with another career decision to make.

After several months, I confided in my good friend and colleague, the human resources (HR) manager of the company, that I had had enough at the aviation company and decided to put a game plan together for my exit strategy. The HR manager understood my frustration. I updated my résumé and let friends and colleagues know that I was in the market for a new job. But until I left the current position, I was committed to the company and would give one hundred percent of my time and talents to my job.

Do what you have to do
until you can do what you want to do.

—Oprah Winfrey

Again, I was fortunate. After several months of searching for a new position, a manufacturing company hired me as controller. My new job satisfied me. I performed new tasks and implemented tools I had learned over the years.

My career was going well, so I decided to get active and volunteer my time, talents, and treasures. I chose the National Association of Black Accountants (NABA). I had already been acquainted with NABA through networking. I realized later that volunteering with NABA was the best decision I could have made, not only from a personal standpoint but also from a career standpoint.

Having been with the manufacturing company for only eight months I had made great progress in my position. I had worked on changing systems and creating a teamwork atmosphere. I was satisfied, happy, and enjoyed the work. I was not in halftime; I was not in the market for a new job. But I found myself being offered a once-in-a-lifetime experience through my acquaintances in NABA.

As I mentioned earlier, when I was at the manufacturing company, an acquaintance in NABA, called to tell me he had referred me to the Miami Dolphins for the controller's position, the same position my colleague and friend, also from NABA and who I had just had lunch with, had interviewed for. But I was selected and I accepted. The toughest part of accepting that job was I already had a good job and my friend was unemployed. I felt bad for my friend, but I believe whatever God has for us, individually, is for us alone, and no one on earth can take that away. I had to accept the fact that God had planned for me to get the job.

The first year with the Miami Dolphins, my job demanded less of me than I had anticipated. With the Dolphins, I worked at a much slower pace than I had been used to at the aviation and the manufacturing companies. This surprised me because of the high energy of the game of football.

My two previous jobs had required high energy with lots of complicated accounting issues. With the Dolphins, I accounted for only ten home games; whereas, in the manufacturing company I had just left, I had accounted for millions of widgets.

I wanted more interesting work to do but thought it would be frowned upon if I spoke up to management. So instead of addressing the issue with my supervisors, I thought it would be better to just look for another job where I would be busier and more fulfilled. So after the first year with the Dolphins—unthinkable, I know—I found myself at halftime working for the National Football League.

I love the game of football. As an eight-year-old girl, I played wide-receiver for our neighborhood co-ed football team—tag football but football nonetheless. For non-football lovers, a wide receiver is usually the fastest person on the team. I was fast. In fact, I had run on the high school track team, and in college, I worked in the athletic department my entire four-years and favored football over other college games.

So one year into the NFL with Miami, I was at halftime once again in my career with a decision to make: Do I want to stay in the prestigious NFL or work in corporate America? I decided not to ask God for direction this time. I already had the answer for what was best for my career. Or so I thought. In fact, I had made the ultimate decision that I wanted to work in corporate America again without discussing it with Him or anyone. I made the decision based on my previous experience working in a fast-paced, high-energy environment. Time to create a new game-plan for my exit strategy. But I needed more information.

I researched and learned that it would be easier, as an accountant, to find a job in corporate America with a master's in business administration (MBA) than with a bachelor's degree in accounting alone. I had already earned my CPA designation, but I knew I would be more marketable with an MBA. So I developed a plan to get my MBA and work for International

Business Machines Corporation (IBM). I had set my goal and created my game plan.

I enrolled in the executive MBA program at Nova Southeastern University in Davie, Florida. The Miami Dolphins had collaborated with Nova in developing the Miami Dolphins Training Facility on the main campus of Nova Southeastern University, so I felt sure of my decision for the institution.

A year and a half later, I received my MBA from Nova.

After graduation, I returned to asking God for direction. Do I stay in the NFL or work in corporate America? I'm sure God thought that was funny because, even when I thought I had controlled my decisions, He had been directing me all along the way. God's direction for me this time: "Wait."

So that's what I did.

By my second year as the controller for the Miami Dolphins and Joe Robbie Stadium, I hadn't done much with the stadium side of the business, however, I reported to both the Dolphins and the stadium executives. Six months after receiving my MBA, my boss at Joe Robbie Stadium resigned. The general manager for both entities, Miami Dolphins and Joe Robbie Stadium, approached me about becoming the next treasurer for the stadium. I said yes, of course, but I wanted a new title. "Vice president of finance and administration" had a nice ring to it and would give me a new identity instead of following after my predecessor with the title of "treasurer."

I was glad that I had asked God for direction and that He had controlled my career move. At the time, I thought that with my MBA degree I would be leaving the NFL for a career in corporate America. I had even made a game plan. But that's just it. It was my game plan—not His.

God will ensure my success
in accordance with His plan, not mine.

—Francis Chan, *Until Unity*

In less than a year as vice president of finance and administration for Joe Robbie Stadium, the team and stadium were sold to (the late) Wayne Huizenga, Sr.

Huizenga had founded Waste Management and AutoNation; he also owned the then-Blockbuster Video. Prior to Huizenga's purchase, Joe Robbie's family had owned the team and stadium; and the business had been run like a family-owned business. But under Huizenga's ownership, a businessman and entrepreneur would be taking over.

Starting my new position at Joe Robbie Stadium, I was nervous and excited at the same time. But I was up for the challenge. Just as I expected, doing business with Wayne Huizenga looked much different than doing business with the Robbie Family. Right away, we updated and converted the general ledger accounting system. This excited me. I had experienced accounting-system conversions during my prior employment with *The Baltimore Sun* and the aviation company. At the direction of Huizenga's leadership team, monthly financial meetings were scheduled with Huizenga, himself, and the president of Huizenga's Holding Company.

Along with taking over the Dolphins and the stadium, Huizenga had purchased a baseball franchise. He named it the "Florida Marlins." The Marlins began playing baseball at Joe Robbie Stadium in 1993. And the challenge was back. Instead of overseeing ten games for the Dolphins, under Huizenga's ownership, I oversaw eighty-one home games for the Marlins—all played in the stadium. In addition, the stadium hosted other events such as concerts, major league soccer, and the Orange Bowl; and the financial responsibility fell to me. I felt fulfilled and as busy as I wanted to be.

A couple of years later, I burned out from the fast-paced stadium events. Note to self: Be careful what you ask God for because you just may get it! I wanted to get back into working for the team side of the NFL rather than the stadium side. I found myself at halftime again. I needed a new game plan. I knew a new plan would lead me out of Miami because the current treasurer for the Miami Dolphins was not leaving anytime soon. So I came up with another game plan for my career. This time I did what I normally do and asked God for direction. And I listened to Him. I trusted in God's will for my life.

I had stayed in touch with my former boss at Robbie Stadium, who by then was working for the NFL front office in New York. I shared with him my desire to leave the stadium business and find a job with a team. Months later, I received a call from my former boss who told me the Los Angeles Rams were moving to St. Louis. He asked me if I was interested in the vice president of finance position; he also asked me to send him my résumé. On faith, not knowing anything about St. Louis, I sent Bill my résumé. Later, I received a call from the Rams. I interviewed and got the job.

After one year with the St. Louis Rams, it felt like déjà vu all over again. Boredom had re-established itself in my job and I considered leaving. But where would I go and what I would do? I put a game plan together on how to motivate myself and remain fulfilled in my job. I had to pivot, and my game plan worked. I created new opportunities for myself to keep me interested in my role as vice president of finance. But then after almost twelve years with the Rams, I felt in my spirit it was time, again, to develop a game plan for my next career move.

During this particular halftime, I did something I had never done before. In the past, I had normally thought and prayed about what I wanted. But this time I was nervous about leaving the Rams after almost twelve years, so I thought I had better do what I tell others to do. I wrote down my goals on paper.

Your goals are the road maps that guide you and show you what is possible for your life.

—Les Brown, motivational/inspirational speaker

In 2004, I wrote my goals down the old fashion way. Instead of using a computer, I pulled out one of my journals and wrote down four goals I wanted to achieve for my career and life. In *Put Your Dream to the Test: 10 Questions to Help You See It and Seize It* (2011), author John Maxwell writes about "The Dream Test." He offers ten questions to answer to help see and seize the dream. My answers to his questions led me to rule out my ultimate goal of owning my own day spa. I discovered I was not willing to pay the price for my dream. I created new goals for my next endeavor. I wrote the following:

1. Stay working in the NFL as CFO
2. Live in the mountains
3. Make X amount in salary
4. Find a great church home

I also wrote down my prayer for my husband to find a great job.

Before I left the Rams in 2007, I sat in my office talking with my assistant, Rosalind. I told her it was time for me to look into my next career opportunity; I wanted something more challenging. I told her I was getting bored.

"Turn around and look out the window," she said.

I did and saw the Rams practice field where the players were practicing, with the fresh green color of the field, the bright white yard lines, and the shirtless players.

She said, "Are you sure you want to give up this cushy job?"

For a second, I actually thought about her words but deep down inside, I knew it was time to leave.

We don't grow when things are easy,
we grow when we face challenges.

—(Anonymous)

In early 2007, a colleague told me about the CFO for the Arizona Cardinals football team retiring. I asked my colleague to make a call to the president of the team.

"I will when I have time," he said.

Unfortunately, I didn't have time to waste, so I went to my office and emailed the president of the team myself, telling him I was interested in the CFO position. Upon his request, I sent him my résumé and was scheduled for an interview. Later they offered me the job of CFO for the Arizona Cardinals.

It was just three years earlier, in 2004, when I had written down my four goals. By the time I started my CFO position with the Cardinals, I had accomplished all four of my goals: 1) I was a CFO in the NFL, 2) living in the mountains, something I had dreamed of since I was in my twenties after a ski trip, 3) being offered the exact salary I had written down in my journal, and 4) finding a church we loved.

My husband and I arrived in Phoenix in June 2007 when the temperature hit about 110 degrees. I knew that would be a problem. I do not like the heat. But my husband fell in love with the city. Two months later, we found our church home! Later my new boss assisted my husband with finding the best job of his career to that point. Not only had my four goals been accomplished, but also my prayer for my husband had been answered. Life was good.

I cannot stress enough the importance of writing down our goals. Writing down goals or dreams holds us accountable.

Most of us have heard about "SMART" goals. SMART goals are Specific, Measurable, Attainable, Relevant, and Time-based (SMART). I'm not sure how smart my goal was to live in Phoenix with temperatures exceeding 110 degrees during the summer months. But the thing with working in the front office of the NFL, we don't always get to choose where the opportunity arises; we just have to make the decision. If it's right, we go for it. Part of the equation of having a successful career includes knowing that nothing is ever perfect, but we will never know unless we try.

The Three Cs of Life: Choices, Chances, Changes.
You must make a choice to take a chance or your life may never change.

—Anonymous

I had taken a chance and made the choice to leave a safe, comfortable, and "cushy job," as my assistant had called it, with the Rams. I had chosen to move to Phoenix for a job that I felt would give me a new and exciting start to the end of my career in the NFL. I had planned to retire with the Arizona Cardinals football team.

In his heart a man plans his course,
but the Lord determines his steps.

—Proverbs 16:9 (NIV)

The Arizona Cardinals turned out not to be a good fit for me. Clearly, God did not plan for me to retire while there. So my career game plan needed to change, but I was not quite sure in what direction.

For the first time in a long time, I had no game plan, no strategy. I continued working for the Cardinals, knowing I needed to create an exit strategy, but I didn't know where to start. The one thing I knew: Going back to my early career goal, I wanted to do something to contribute to the well-being of women and girls.

During this particular half-time experience, while considering what to do if I left the Arizona Cardinals, I prayed and asked God for direction. Remember that powerful duo, fear and doubt? I said that fear and doubt together can stop you in your place. Well, I definitely experienced both. I stayed in what I called my "valley experience" and did nothing to bring about my next career change…then I received the call that changed my life.

My dear friend Toni called me about the open position of CEO at YWCA Metro St. Louis. I applied, interviewed, was offered, and accepted the new position back in St. Louis. I'd be working for an agency that works toward eliminating racism and empowering women. I was not only going to work for a women and girls' organization, but I'd be fulfilling my personal mission in life: inspiring and enhancing the lives of women and girls!

My husband, as always, supported my career change. We were moving back to St. Louis.

Along with holding us accountable, I believe writing down goals and not just speaking them gives us the motivation we need to execute and implement our strategy to accomplish our dreams.

Write it down. Written goals have a way of
transforming wishes into wants;
can'ts into cans; dreams into plans; plans into reality.
Don't just think it—ink it.

—Michael Korda, *With Wings Like Eagles: A History of the Battle of Britain*

Chapter Four:

Game Time – Do You Have the Right People on Your Team?

Winning or losing depends on having the right people.

—Greg Smith, keynote speaker,consultant, trainer

No matter what kind of business you are in, whether sports, corporate, nonprofit, government, or other, having the right people on your team determines success or failure. In my experience, building the team sometimes is more challenging than the work itself. I found this to be true primarily due to the diversity of the team. We all have differences of opinions, work ethics, backgrounds, values, communication skills, work experience, team-building experiences, and so on. Another challenge I experienced as a leader was not just building the team but also keeping the team together. Most CEOs will admit that without our people, we could not achieve our goals.

You don't build a business; you build people and then the people build the business.

—Zig Ziglar, *Born to Win: Find Your Success Code*

So how do we build a winning team? I remember my days as vice president of finance for the St. Louis Rams. Coach Dick Vermeil always said everyone in the organization was important to the success on the field. Leaders set the culture of the organization, and Coach Vermeil did just that.

After winning Super Bowl XXXIV, everyone in the organization received a Super-Bowl ring. For some NFL teams, only the executive team gets Super-Bowl rings after winning a Super Bowl. But not at the Rams. From the least to the greatest, we were all treated as valuable members of the team. Coach Vermeil not only talked the talk, but he also walked the walk. He knew some of the important ingredients of building a strong team: making members feel appreciated, valued, heard, and respected. In the book, *Everybody Matters* (2016), Bob Chapman says that leadership cultivates a dynamic, trust-building enviro nment that brings out the best in everyone and inspires pride.

Let's start with building a team. I believe building a strong team begins with the leader. My husband likes to use the phrase, "Speed of the leader, speed of the team." During his sales career in corporate America, leadership training was part of the culture. When we first met, positive affirmations adorned his office. I loved them then, and he continues to regularly feed me with positive quotes, such as, "Achieve success through a positive mental attitude (PMA)"; "Have courage to face the truth"; "You can do it if you believe you can"; "Be willing to risk failure in order to succeed"; and "Direct your thoughts, control your emotions, ordain your destiny."

When I decided to write this book, I thought it would be a good idea for me to speak with one of the greatest leaders I know—Coach Dick Vermeil—to get his advice on leadership.

I'll never forget it. We were attending Isaac Bruce's gala in 2019, celebrating the twentieth anniversary of the St. Louis Ram's Super Bowl XXXIV win. It was a great event with more than 300 attendees. Many of the "1999 Greatest Show on Turf" players and coaches were in attendance. I had a chance to speak and take pictures with many of them.

That night, I asked the one and only Coach Vermeil for his advice. We stepped aside to be alone so I could express my desire to write a book on leadership and include his advice. I felt confident in my knowledge of the ins and outs of leadership; after all, I had just received my certification as a John Maxwell certified leadership coach, trainer, and speaker.

So just me and Coach Vermeil standing on the side during the gala. I said, "Coach, will you be my mentor as I write this book on leadership?" For three years working with Coach at the Rams, he had always been willing whenever I asked him to support a particular event or initiative I was involved in. So I expected him to say, "Sure, of course I will." Instead, the first thing he said was, "Why do you want to write another book on leadership? There are so many books out there already. What will make your book different from the others?"

At that time, I had no answer. I had no clarity on how my book would be different from the others.

He said, "Just call me when you're ready to start."

At first, I thought, *He's right. Why should I write another book on leadership? How would my book be different from the others?* For over a year, I pondered his question. Through that year, I never called Coach Vermeil. I was lost. I had spent thousands of dollars in my quest to write a book but each time I started the first chapter—which by the way, I attempted three times—nothing made sense. I thought it would be easy. After all, I'm a leader, so how hard could it be to write on leadership?

But my negative thoughts kept me from writing the book. I had said for so long "I'm not a writer" that I began to believe it. I had embedded the thought so deeply I had everyone else believing it too. Even after becoming CEO for YWCA St. Louis, I wrote short articles or letters which our PR manager always edited and made changes to anyway so, subconsciously, I did not put my soul into my writing. I contemplated hiring a ghostwriter for my book. I had convinced myself that I was not a writer.

Confidence is a habit that can be developed
by acting as if you already had the confidence
you desire to have.

—Brian Tracy, *The Phoenix Transformation*

To be a good leader, one of the main ingredients is to have confidence in yourself and your abilities. *Speed of the leader, speed of the team.* For the Rams to win the Super Bowl, Coach Vermeil first had to believe they could and then show the team the confidence necessary to achieve it. Even a good leader may need to hire a coach for encouragement sometimes, which is what I did and why I'm finally writing my book. I wanted to believe I could do it, but having my coach, Edie Varley, there to encourage me and build my confidence was a blessing.

Today, as I write this book, it has been almost two years since my conversation with Coach Vermeil. I can finally answer his question as to why I want to write a book on leadership and what will make it different from all the others. I believe all leaders have a story to tell; and even though we've been through similar or maybe the same experiences, we all have a unique DNA that makes our delivery different. And nobody can tell your story the way you can. My hope in writing this book is to add value to the lives of others and give them the courage to tell their story.

Sometime as leaders, we don't always get the opportunity to select our team, instead we inherit the team. Other times, we get to build our team from ground zero. As I look back over my career, I have never had the opportunity to build a team from ground zero. I always inherited at least one player on my teams. Rarely does a football head coach build his team from ground zero. It varies, but usually a coach will inherit at least twenty or more players on a team.

As a leader, building a team starts from within. What I mean by that is, when we live from the inside out, we are not easily influenced by the outside world but by the innate person we are. I believe the inside job of the leader or coach starts with personal values. Whether the team is inherited or not, the values of the leader usually determine the culture of the team. Some values or qualities, in my opinion, should be inherent in all great leaders, such as integrity, confidence, decisiveness, empathy, excellence, and transparency. There are many more values that I can list, but for me, these are the top values of leaders who create a winning team. I believe that I possess these qualities today. However, if I may be vulnerable with you, I have not always demonstrated all of these qualities.

As a CPA, integrity held the number one spot for me as the value that all leaders should possess. Empathy, excellence, and transparency come naturally to me. I have never struggled with those values. However, I had to develop confidence and decisiveness. For me, they are like muscles that I had to constantly work to build up; they did not come easily. As I look back over my life, many variables created weaknesses. I am not alone. What I know for sure, some of our greatest leaders lacked confidence and decisiveness at times. They didn't let these deficits stop them in their path to success though. They found a way to overcome, conquer, and strengthen their weaknesses.

Confidence is not something that blooms overnight.
It takes time to develop.

—Anne Hathaway, Actor

This quote resonates with me on many levels. For one, it confirms my faith that we can overcome our weaknesses with practice and patience. As a leader, there were times when I wasn't sure the decision I wanted to make was the right one, but I had to make the decision and have faith that things would turn out right. Sometimes it did and sometimes it did not. I've learned as a leader, though, that one way or the other, we have to make the decision and deal with the outcome.

When building a team, we don't know at the time whether we've made the right hires. And in business, there is no training camp like in football. In football, the coach has the opportunity during training camp to evaluate the talent of each player. If the player does not perform to the standards required, the player is cut, usually without retaliation. However, business leaders are sometimes afraid to fire an employee for fear of employee retaliation, such as filing a grievance or, even worse, filing an EEOC claim or lawsuit for wrongful termination. I have had successful and unsuccessful hires. In addition, I have inherited good team players and bad team players. This is where it gets tough.

Just like football, business leaders must determine from the interviewing process who they feel will make a good addition to the team. Unlike football, leaders are not looking for the physical abilities, like running a 4.4 or how many tackles, blocks, or catches the person has made. Instead, they're looking at the candidate's experience and trying to figure out if they have the right values that would fit into the culture of the organization and the team.

My husband and I had dinner at a restaurant one night and the service was amazing. Not once did we want for anything. Our table seemed to be the responsibility of the entire team and not just one person. When our water ran low, someone stopped by to refill our glasses. And it wasn't the same person every time. Whoever saw the glass empty refilled the glasses. Just like that. It was automatic. I noticed the same behavior the entire evening from each employee. Every so often, a different server checked on us to make sure we didn't need anything. I'm used to having just one person wait on me and not the entire team. At the end of our dinner, the manager came to our table to ask how the meal was. I told him the meal was great but the most impressive experience I had was the way the team of servers attended to me and my husband. I asked the manager, "How is it that your entire team seems to be working as one big happy family?"

He said, "When we hire, we don't hire solely on experience. That's only part of the equation and not always the most important part." He continued, "For us, it's important to hire the person with the right attitude and the right values that will fit into our culture. We can train a person to be a waiter or waitress, but we can't train a person to have the values and attitude that will fit into the culture."

That was evident to me and my husband. It was as if all the employees had the same DNA, which was to provide excellent customer service.

On a team, it's not the strength of the individual players, but it is the strength of the unit and how they all function together.

—Bill Belichick, head coach, New England Patriots

While I was at the Rams, Coach Vermeil would always tell us, "The whole is greater than the sum of all its parts." I found that to be true when working on a team. As we know, there is no "I" in team. When I'm looking to build a team, like the restaurant manager, I look for the individual that has the qualities that will complement the culture of the team.

I have shared with you the qualities I believe are important for any leader; i.e., integrity, confidence, decisiveness, empathy, excellence, and transparency. Certain characteristics should be evident in a successful and effective team as well. Some of the top characteristics for a team in my mind include clear communication with each other, diversity of the group, trust, orientation towards goals, mutual support, ability to perform respective duties, accountability, standards of excellence, respect for each other, and collaboration. I wish I could tell you that every team I have ever managed possessed all the characteristics I just listed, but that would be a lie. Unfortunately, I have managed a couple of dysfunctional teams in my career. If I had to tell you in which areas the teams fell short, I would have to say, first, lack of trust and, second, inability to perform duties.

Trust is knowing that when a team member does push you, they're doing it because they care about the team.

—Patrick Lencioni, *The Motive: Why So Many Leaders Abdicate Their Most Important Responsibilities*

The thing is, each team member is responsible for performing their respective job. Sometime it takes the whole team's help and support to ensure each member lives up to their responsibility. Like the restaurant manager I spoke about earlier, when I have a team member that's struggling with their task and they have the right attitude and values that benefit the organization and the team, my first attempt is to give that member support. I ask other team members for ideas and suggestions on how we can help the one who's struggling. This happened early in my career.

As a new manager, I hired a person who was not catching on to the job as quickly as I had hoped. She became very close to another team member. The team member knew the struggle of this employee and came to me to ask, "How can I help?" I explained what we needed as a team and my expectations. Within a month, the struggling team member began to improve and she turned things around.

I can do things you cannot; you can do things I cannot; together we can do great things.

—Mother Teresa

I have had my challenges as a leader when things didn't go so well, when teams did not get along and I did not always have the right people on the team. Conflict occurred most in those scenarios. I have experienced conflict at some level throughout my career either as a leader or as a team member. In some instances, I've been very successful in resolving conflict as the leader. However, in other instances, I have not been as successful; and quite frankly, the conflict resulted in total disaster.

As a leader, I learned lessons and/or strategies necessary for successful conflict resolutions, including: 1) having an awareness that conflict exists within the team, 2) listening effectively, 3) demonstrating empathy for others, 4) practicing respect for team members, 5) gaining knowledge of the facts, 6) communicating effectively, 7) determining the reason for the conflict, and 8) finding a solution. There are many more strategies to resolve conflict at work, but these strategies most effectively worked for me.

The first critical lesson a leader should learn: awareness. If a leader is not aware of the conflict, then nothing will change. When conflict is embraced, it provides an environment for positive change. Unfortunately, some leaders are not always willing to embrace or even admit conflict exists within the team.

If you avoid conflict to keep the peace,
you start a war inside yourself.

—Cheryl Richardson, *The Art of Extreme Self-Care Revised Edition: 12 Practical and Inspiring Ways to Love Yourself More*

I recall a time when I ignored a conflict within my team. I had been working on the job for only a couple of months and had picked up on friction right away. I did not want to deal with it at that moment. I felt that if I just ignored the problem, it would magically go away. I had hoped the two leaders involved could work it out on their own and come to a peaceful reconciliation. Well, it did not turn out that way and eventually turned into a nightmare. I decided to stop ignoring the problem because it was not going to resolve by itself. So I called a meeting with the two parties. For the first two minutes, calmness reigned—of course, that was during the time I was speaking. Once I opened the meeting up for discussion, it became chaotic. Each person blamed the other. After ten minutes, I ended the conversation knowing that nothing good could come out of it. For starters, none of the strategies I listed above worked: No self-awareness existed for either party, no listening to the other person, no empathy, no respect for the other person, no willingness to understand the facts from one another, no effective communication, no desire to discuss the reason for the conflict, and no interest in finding a solution.

Not everything that is faced can be changed.
But nothing can be changed until it is faced.

—James Baldwin, *The Price of the Ticket: Collected Nonfiction: 1948–1985*

From that first conflict experience, among other things, I had to face that my team members lacked trust in each other. In my opinion, trust is the foundation of a good team. Patrick Lencioni's book, *The Five Dysfunctions of a Team* (2013), confirmed for me that the number one dysfunction of a team is the "absence of trust."

After speaking with the two parties, individually, I realized they felt threatened by the other. To make things worse, they simply did not like each other. In sports, this is not uncommon. Players don't always agree, or even like each other for that matter; but when the game is on the line, they find a way to put aside their differences for the good of the team. I have witnessed this first-hand.

Working in the NFL for over eighteen years, I had the opportunity to speak one-on-one with players. One player affirmed what I had experienced as a leader; that is, that one of the main reasons a player lacks trust in his teammate is the ongoing inability of the teammate to do their job.

The team's trust in a player will diminish if the player does not live up to expectations. In football, if a running back continues to fumble the ball, the coach will bench him. If this player continues to fumble over time, the coach and the team will lose trust in the player. Usually, if this continues to happen, the coach will cut the player. If the coach doesn't cut the player, the other players may become frustrated and conflict will eventually creep in. The performance of that player will likely affect the performance of the team as a whole—not only on the field but in the locker room as well. When the team breaks down in this manner, it's time for the coach to decide whether or not to cut the player. Like football, in business, once we lose trust within our team, a winning team becomes nearly impossible to build or rebuild.

Earlier I talked about a restaurant manager who hired his employees primarily for their attitude and values, not just their skills. Well, in sports and business, that's not always the case. Coaches and business leaders don't always have the luxury of keeping a team member on the team because of their positive attitude; however, it does happen occasionally. I know of a basketball player who is well past his prime, but his positive mental attitude is needed for his young teammates to whom he is considered a mentor. In business, if a team member does not perform to the degree needed to get the job done, despite their positive attitude, that team member must be terminated for the good of the team.

Talent wins games, but teamwork and intelligence wins championships.

—Michael Jordan, professional basketball player, businessman

Have you ever had an employee who you knew was not a good fit for your team but you kept them on nonetheless? I have. As leaders, why do we keep that employee knowing that our team will not achieve the success it's capable of achieving? I have had team members that did not perform up to expectations, but I did not terminate them. When I look back as to why, there were many reasons. One in particular is called "emotional hostage." An emotional-hostage situation arises when someone acts in a malicious, vindictive, or manipulative manner and causes emotional pain to another.

I experienced this emotional-hostage phenomenon during the course of my career. I did not terminate the employee due to fear (False Evidence Appearing Real). Sometimes we believe that if we fire the employee, no one else will be able to do the job. We also fear retaliation from the employee. So we remain in an emotion-hostage situation, afraid to make that difficult decision of letting go. In most cases, when we don't sever the ties, it creates a negative work environment. That negative atmosphere will permeate the team until the team becomes dysfunctional. The trust is broken.

Many reasons to avoid conflict exist. For me, I did not want to tell my employee the truth about how I felt about their performance. I once had a boss who told me exactly how he felt about my performance and it crushed me, so I never wanted to make anyone feel that way. For several months, I lamented over his words and allowed them to make me feel less than competent. But when I look back at what my boss said to me at that time, I believe he meant no harm. He needed me to improve in certain areas, not only for me but also for the best interest of the company. Then I did what I usually do: I prayed to God asking for strength and direction.

The way of a fool seems right to him,
but a wise man listens to advice.

—Proverbs 12:15 (NIV)

The message came. I picked myself up by the bootstraps and took the advice of my boss. I worked on an improvement plan. That tough lesson propelled my career.

With hindsight, I learned the importance of having and communicating clear expectations from that experience. I learned my boss expected one thing and I interpreted something different. That type of misinterpretation or miscommunication by either party may wreak havoc on a team.

When a quarterback calls a passing play in the huddle, he expects the wide receiver to be at a certain spot when he throws the ball. But if the quarterback throws to the right and the player runs to the left, that miscommunication can cause a major conflict in the team, especially if it continues to happen over time. All players on the team, in football and business, must have clear expectations of his or her role. As my coach, Edie, says, "The root of all conflict is unmet expectations."

In football, if the player cannot perform the expectations of the position, the coach is forced to terminate the player's contract. The same is true in business. If the team player cannot perform their job, the leader must document and sever ties sooner than later. If not, the team will suffer, eventually becoming dysfunctional and unproductive.

The advice I leave for new leaders is the old saying, "Hire slow but fire fast." This rings very true when we don't have the right team members. In the long run, having the right team members will make life a lot easier and the team more productive.

The most important thing you do as a leader
is to hire the right people.
—David Cottrell, *The First Two Rules of Leadership*

Chapter Five:

Time Management – Increase Your Effectiveness, Efficiency, and Productivity

Time flies. It's up to you to be the navigator.

—Robert Orben, comedy writer,
former speechwriter, magician

Time management is a key component to winning for any sports team. The same is true in business and our personal lives. I've struggled with time management throughout my life, both career-wise and personally.

What is time management? On the Corporate Finance Institute website, they say that time management is taking control of the time you've planned for specific activities. If done right, good time management will lead to efficiency, productivity, and a less-stressed, more successful life (CFI, 2021). Why is time management important? For me it's simple. We are limited to twenty-four hours in a day and the effective use of that limited time is vital to success.

When I worked in the NFL, I paid close attention to how coaches managed their timeouts. I knew timeouts stopped the play and the clock. I also knew timeouts may be called for necessary or strategic reasons. For example, the coach or quarterback will call a necessary timeout to attend to an injured player, stop the clock, and avoid a penalty when the game clock is winding down to zero. Teams may also strategize to force a timeout and stop the clock, such as:

- a player running the ball out of bounds
- the quarterback spiking the ball on the ground
- the quarterback throwing the ball out of bounds
- the team waiting for the two-minute warning

When I watch a game and the coach calls a timeout that I think is not necessary, I scream, "You're wasting a timeout." Why am I so upset? Because in football, managing time could be the difference between a win or a loss. Professional NFL football allows only six timeouts in the entire game; therefore—in my opinion, anyway—timeouts should be a time-management strategy.

Timeouts stop the clock from ticking. Why is this important? When the clock stops ticking, it gives the team time to set up their defensive- or offensive-play calls. Wouldn't it be great if we could stop the clock to allow time for us to accomplish whatever we've set out to do?

Since we cannot stop time, though, we must create time management strategies in our lives that allow us to accomplish our goals. First, let's look at some of the reasons why we don't seem to have enough time:

- We are easily distracted.
- We don't get enough rest.
- We are not organized.

- We don't have outlined specific goals for the day, week, or month.
- We have not prioritized.
- We have ineffectively scheduled calendar items.
- We spend too much time checking emails throughout the day.

Many more reasons exist, of course, for why we may not have enough time, but I've struggled with the reasons above in my life. As I look at some of these reasons, I realize an NFL player or any professional athlete would probably lose their job under these circumstances.

What distracts us will begin to define us.
We don't have to swing at every pitch.
—Bob Goff, *Dream Big: Know What You Want, Why You Want It, and What You're Going to Do About It*

We Are Easily Distracted

So what's keeping you from accomplishing your goals and/or checking "done" on your to-do list? Like I said earlier, all of the above reasons kept me from writing this book. I spent thousands of dollars on coaches to help motivate me. It wasn't until my husband, Vito, said, "You've got everything within you to write your book. Why are you giving your money away when you already know what you have to do? Just write the darn book."

Well, that sounded good. But guess what. I still didn't write the darn book. The truth is, I allowed distractions to get in my way. As leaders, we must stay focused on the task at hand; otherwise, we are less productive, less effective, and less efficient.

I've been called a "Type A" personality by some of my colleagues. My assistant at the YWCA, Anita, said, "Mrs. Bracy, I feel like I'm on roller skates with you, trying to keep up." At first, I laughed, but then I realized she was right. I routinely began a new task before I finished the task at hand. Some days, I asked her to do seven tasks within a span of a few hours. I felt like a hamster on a wheel with no end in sight. That's when I decided to hire—yes—another coach. This time, a time management coach.

Jill Farmer authored *There's Not Enough Time...and Other Lies We Tell Ourselves* (2012). For me, the money I spent on her coaching was well worth it. For the first time in my life, I was reporting to someone on managing my time. I have to admit. At first, I felt uncomfortable because I did not want to be accountable to anyone for my time—after all, it was *my time*. But I learned many lessons from Jill. Grant you, I already knew some of those lessons but didn't practice them. Embarrassing! It took hearing them from Jill to have them sink into my head. In her book, I love the two chapters on to-do-list makeovers. Tool No. 4 especially spoke to me: Prioritizing. As I read about the different prioritization zones, it was no surprise to me that I was in the "hamster-on-the-wheel" zone.

The hamster-on-the-wheel zone described me perfectly: lots of interruptions, some phone calls, constant checking my emails, meetings all day, and some pressing matters. People in this zone stay in constant movement, always busy. At times, I'm so busy being busy I am exhausted by the time I get around to doing the task I had planned to complete. As Jill would say, "We're constantly moving and not going anywhere" (Farmer, 27).

Today, I have to be intentional about staying focused and not allowing distractions to take me off my game. My husband often tells me that I don't know how to stop being busy. He's right. I often feel guilty if I'm not busy doing something—anything.

"I wish I could turn that energy into exercising, but I'm too busy, not enough time," I say.

Does that sound familiar? I'm sure you know people who use that excuse for not exercising. I used "not enough time," too, as an excuse for not exercising.

Can you imagine if Kurt Warner, former quarterback for the Super Bowl Champions St. Louis Rams, said to Coach Vermeil, "Sorry, Coach, I don't have enough time to do my workouts." I can tell you right now, Kurt would not have a job. Actually, I can say, if any player said he didn't have time to do mandatory workouts, he would be cut from the team. Being a Super Bowl champ requires a winning mindset and managing time is a characteristic of a winner!

In 2019, I told everyone who would listen that 2020 was my year of no. I had made a decision that I would NOT say yes to every invitation I received. I was tired of hamster-wheeling. I wanted to take back my time and stop giving it away to people who didn't know or care about me. Prior to 2020, I attended every gala event I was invited to. Why did I have to attend everything?

My niece, who is a generation millennial, told me that I had "FOMO" (fear of missing out.) She's probably right. But I did not want to hurt friends by not attending a gala or disappoint my colleagues for not participating as a panelist in one of their women events. I said yes to ninety percent of the people who asked me to do something. I began to feel resentment. Instead of enjoying the events, I felt overwhelmed. That's when I knew it was time to stop wearing myself out to please everyone else but me. I wanted my time back so I could enjoy my husband and do things I wanted to do. I know from experience that to stop being busy when you are fixated on it is tough.

I have used the word "intentional" a few times in this book. That's because, for me, I have to be intentional about changing habits that I have lived with all my adult life—and saying yes is one of them. When I made the statement in 2019 that 2020 would be my year of saying no, I had no clue we would be hit by the 2020 pandemic. The virus put an end to my in-person business; however, it did not stop the busyness. Meeting face-to-face became meeting virtually. So I had to be intentional about saying no to all of the Zoom invites I received on a daily basis. It's still not easy, but I'm taking it one day at a time.

Give yourself permission to say no
without feeling guilty, mean, or selfish...
Be at peace with your decisions.

—Stephanie Lahart, *Before You Commit: Powerful, Unfiltered,*and *Thought-Provoking Relationship Advice for Single Women*

We Don't Get Enough Rest

Feeling exhausted is a legitimate reason why we fail to manage our time. In 2013, the last year measured by Gallup, the average American slept 6.8 hours a night with forty percent reporting less than six hours of sleep. Why? Because we live in a 24/7 society. Our minds constantly work. There is always something to do; our work is never done. I struggle in this area, especially during this time of a global health crisis. At night, I find it easy to fall asleep but hard to stay asleep. By three a.m., I wake up thinking about my to-do list. I start planning for the day's meetings; I remember emails I forgot to reply to or emails I never had a chance to open. The list is long, and I stay awake until five a.m. planning it all in my mind. Then I dose off, and the alarm clock goes off at six a.m. I'm exhausted the entire day, less productive, and fail to complete my to-do list. By the time I get home from work, I have no energy for my family. I eat dinner late, spend an hour or so with my husband, prepare for bed, and start the routine all over again.

During my career in the NFL, I heard about a player who fell asleep watching a video of the opponent. Why? Because he did not get enough rest. An athlete cannot perform, mentally or physically, at an optima level without enough sleep.

As leaders, we must take care of ourselves and find ways to ensure we get enough rest. So when I became sick and tired of being sick and tired, I did something about it. I changed my routine by exercising, eating right, meditating, and going to spa treatments, hoping to count on several techniques that would help me regain control of my lack of sleep. I started sleeping at least seven hours a night; I was less tired during the day and more productive.

Getting enough rest gave me the energy I needed to accomplish or exceed my goals. In fact, my assistant, Anita, noticed the difference and sent me another email: "Mrs. Bracy, I'm trying to keep up with you." Anita was still running after me, but I was no longer on the hamster wheel. I was not all over the place, but instead, focused and strategic, which made a huge difference in our productivity. Taking care of ourselves, especially getting enough rest, allows us to perform at an optimal level.

Having peace, happiness and healthiness is my definition of beauty. And you can't have any of that without sleep.

—Beyonce, singer, songwriter

We Are Not Organized

Not being organized is another reason why we feel there is not enough time in the day. I don't know about you, but when I'm not organized, I feel stressed, irritated. I can't find important documents, my keys, my cell phone, the ticket from the cleaners, the book—and the list goes on. How much time can we save by being organized?

Several times in the past, I have spent thirty minutes looking for my keys. If only I had been organized, I would not have been late for work, stressed in traffic, irritated with drivers, and blaming everyone else. Maybe keys aren't the issue for you, but maybe you've misplaced an important document at work. Whatever the case may be, being organized could save us time and bring peace into our lives.

In 2020, during the global pandemic, we could all have used a little peace! Right? So let's get organized and declutter our lives. I have to admit, the older I get, the more important it is for me to be consistent with being organized. In other words, having a special place for my keys, labels for my folders, a specific drawer in the file cabinet for my documents, a designated place for my cell phone, and on and on. It makes my life easier knowing where to find what I'm looking for when I need it. More importantly, it saves time.

We Don't Have Specific Goals for the Day, Week, or Month Outlined

Along with organization, setting goals saves time in our day. Effective goal-setting is one of the most important activities for any leader. In addition, setting goals helps us spend less time making adjustments; instead, we have more time to focus on accomplishing our goals. I have wasted precious hours adjusting goals that were not realistic or, frankly, were not the right goals from the beginning.

Remember the SMART-goal model? "SMART" is an acronym for Specific, Measurable, Achievable, Relevant, and Time-bound. SMART goals may take time planning, but in the long run, utilizing SMART goals will save time and create a more effective and efficient leader.

It's not enough to be busy. So are the ants.
The question is: What are we busy about?

—Henry David Thoreau

We Have Not Prioritized

Like setting goals saves time in our day, prioritizing those goals also saves time. Numerous books and articles exist on prioritization and time management. I have read several for my own personal edification.

As leaders, we sometimes mistake busyness with productivity. We may spend time doing things that give us a false sense of accomplishment. We believe that we're making progress just by being busy. Sometimes if we are busy doing things that we enjoy or things that we just want to check off the to-do list, we think we are doing something meaningful. In fact, those projects steal precious time. We allow these diversions to keep us from achieving our goals for the day. If we want to be successful leaders, we must manage our time because of its preciousness and because we cannot get time back once it's gone.

In the first session with my time-management coach, Jill Farmer, she asked me to write down things or activities that kept me busy. After I finished listing all the things I was involved with, mental exhaustion took over. I realized why I didn't have time to accomplish some of my goals. I realized that besides my career and home life, I volunteered my time in other activities: I served on a couple of nonprofit boards; I chaired a couple of events; and I acted as treasurer for a women's service organization. You get the picture. Most of what I was doing did not bring me joy. I volunteered because someone asked me to, not because I wanted to. You've heard the saying, "If you want something done, give it to a busy person"? That was me. Busy-bee. I would say yes to a friend or colleague and, later, feel resentment for giving up my time for someone else's priorities. Although everything I did was important and made an impact on someone's life, it was not getting me closer to reaching my goals. After sharing this information with Jill, she challenged me to give up anything that was not a priority.

When I first started working with Edie, my executive coach, and shared with her my desire to write a book, I told her all the reasons I did not have time to write. She asked me the same question Jill had asked, "What's keeping you from writing your book?" By that time, I had resigned from many of the extracurricular activities I had been involved with; however, I continued with one. Edie asked why that was. I told her because of relationships. But that wasn't enough of a reason for her. She challenged me to either give up the activity altogether or make it work in my favor. I realized she was right. If the activity brought value to others, it had to bring value to me; otherwise, the activity becomes important but not a priority. I had to say no to some things and yes to things that would bring me closer to achieving my goals. In other words, I had to spend my time wisely! I had to prioritize.

Learn to say "no" to the good
so you can say "yes" to the best.
—John C. Maxwell, *Developing the Leader Within You*

I can't say that I've mastered these areas—that is, being organized, specifying goals, and prioritizing. I still have a long way to go, but I feel good about my progress in being intentional to improve.

We Have Ineffectively Scheduled Calendar Items

Calendar scheduling ranks high as another important area of time management. Calendar scheduling is the art of being intentional about planning your activities so that you can achieve your goals and priorities in the allotted time. When done properly, the benefits can be tremendous. The opposite holds true; i.e., if you do not properly plan your calendar, you can waste a lot of time getting nowhere fast. You can end up at the end of the day spinning your wheels just like that hamster.

Now, let's look at some of the benefits of effective calendaring. Not only does effective calendaring help with time management but it helps with keeping us from embarrassment. For example, as CEO of YWCA, meetings occurred regularly. One day, I had an important meeting with a high-worth donor for YWCA. My calendar indicated the meeting would be held at Restaurant A, so that's where I went. After fifteen minutes, the donor did not arrive. I called the donor. She answered and said, "I'm here waiting for you." During the conversation, I learned that a former assistant (not Anita, this was before Anita) had told the donor Restaurant B and told me Restaurant A. Fortunately, the donor waited while I traveled to Restaurant B.

This improper calendaring could have sabotaged money and time, but fortunately, the donor understood and did not hold this error against YWCA or me. Not only does effective calendaring help with saving time and money but work-life balance as well. There's nothing like having quality time to spend with loved ones.

We Spend Too Much Time Checking Emails Throughout the Day

Checking emails was one of the important discussions I had with my time management coach, Jill Farmer. She asked me in our first or second session how much time I spent on checking and responding to emails. I was embarrassed. I told her I checked my emails every time the notification button popped up on my computer letting me know I'd received a new email.

She said, "First thing you need to do is to turn off the notification button."

The notifications were a nuisance, but I didn't want to miss any important emails. I told you in an earlier chapter about my millennial niece who told me I had FOMO (fear of missing out). That was true in emails as well. The Harvard Business Review (HBR) published the results of a McKinsey analysis in January 2019. It said that over a quarter of employees spend their workday checking and answering emails. I fell into that statistic. Makes me wonder how much time I wasted during the day. The problem is that after checking each email, we lose concentration on the task at hand. In my experience, it could take me at least ten minutes to get back into the groove of what I was doing.

So per Jill's advice, I turned off my notifications and started checking emails only once an hour. I took care of emails right away, if possible, or deleted them; but I didn't leave them in my inbox to take up space. Emails I needed to retain, I moved out of my inbox after reading them and move them into another folder to handle later or to file away. And one last thing I would say about emails, don't waste your time on irrelevant, unimportant emails…delete! By the way, this method works also for inter-office or good old-fashion United States Post Office mail. Now, this system may not work for you but find a system that does work and spend less time checking and dealing with email. I have, by no means, conquered the email area of time management, but I can celebrate that I have come a long way.

One thing that I make time for that is non-negotiable is my morning devotion. Come rain or high water, I always have time to start my day in prayer, meditation, and reading a Bible scripture. My morning ritual does not have to go into my calendar because it's like cement in my heart. On rare days when I don't have time in the morning for my devotional, I'll save it for the evening—but my entire day is off-kilter.

Another thing I have made a priority in my life is watching the sunset with my husband at least three days a week when he's available. Being intentional about time allows us to live life on purpose.

Let's look at another way of thinking about time management.

I read my first professional development book, *The 7 Habits of Highly Effective People* (2013), by Stephen R. Covey, at age twenty-seven. This book changed not only my professional life but also my personal life. In Part Two, Habit Three, "Put First Things First," Covey recognizes that time management is a misnomer, saying that the challenge is not time management but self-management. He goes on to say, "Rather than focusing on things and time, focus on preserving and enhancing relationships and on accomplishing results" (Covey 159). When I first read this chapter, it confused me. I did not understand the concept of managing myself. Growing up, at that time into my twenties, I thought I had to accept my schedule as given by my boss, my family, and/or my friends. I just went with the flow and figured it out along the way. Unfortunately, that thought process became my reality throughout most of my adult life. What was really interesting in reading Covey's book was learning the "The Time Management Matrix" (Covey 2013).

Before reading *Seven Habits*, I thought everything was important and urgent. Throughout my career, I have grasped the importance of understanding the difference between these two concepts. I spent countless hours working on important projects, but like I said earlier, they may not have been a priority. When I followed that pattern, at the end of the day, I did not have enough time to complete the priority projects. After reading *Seven Habits* and many other books on time management and professional development, I was still not able to manage myself. That's how I became a Type A personality and lived on the hamster wheel for so long—again, falling into the trap of saying yes to things that were not important but urgent. I learned that most urgent matters were not my issues but someone else's. As Covey explains, a statement of importance has to do with results. If something is important, it contributes to your mission, your values, or your high-priority objectives. I totally get that now. In the past, I worked on and accomplished urgent matters, but after completing the so-called task, I realized it wasn't important. In other words, it could have waited until after lunch with my husband—a priority.

In the best-selling book *It's About Time: The Art of Choosing the Meaningful Over the Urgent* (2019), author Valorie Burton talks about the art of choosing the meaningful over the urgent. She introduces another tool called the "Time-Meaning Management Matrix" (181). In this exercise, the reader is asked to rate an activity on a scale of one to ten based on the time commitment required for the task. Activities rated six or higher may be considered meaningful and should be accomplished; any activity below a six should be avoided.

Many books and tools exist in the market to help us manage our time; they can be found easily, either online or in bookstores. But at the end of the day, managing time is a choice that each of us can make.

In addition to the skills I've mentioned previously, one of the best leadership skills I learned about time management was the art of effective delegation. Learning to delegate effectively, or giving others the chance to learn and grow, is one of the most powerful high-leveraging activities a leader can do. Many leaders feel it takes too much time and effort to teach someone a task; it's easier for them to do it themselves—and they feel they can do it better than anyone else. But effective leaders delegate. Delegation improves a leader's ability to manage themselves.

To delegate, I had to make the choice to let go of control. I had to learn to trust my team and their abilities to complete an assignment I delegated to them. When I learned the skill of delegating, I was better able to self-manage and gained back precious time in the long run. Not only did I open up more time for myself, but I empowered my staff with development and growth, which, at the end of the day, increased the organization's financial bottom line. When done right, delegation brings about a win-win for the leader, the team, and the team member doing the job.

What helped me with self-management was creating a different mindset. I made an intentional decision that, in order to better manage my time, I had to be disciplined and manage my thoughts about time, also recognize that I had the ability to regulate my thoughts. In Jill Farmer's book, *There's Not Enough Time* (2012), she suggests asking, "What if there is enough time? What happens when you think that thought?" (78). She goes on to say, "Just thinking the thought 'there is enough time,' we trigger a cycle that taps into our most efficient, productive selves. We give ourselves the gift of time" (80). Now that's managing ourselves by taking control of our thoughts. That's an "aha" moment.

If you want to add time to your life, you must first start with your mindset. It's a choice, you get to decide.

—Adrian E. Bracy

Chapter Six:

The Three P's – Purpose, Passion & Potential

Purpose is the reason you journey.
Passion is the fire that lights the way.
Potential is the skill needed to fulfill your purpose.

—Anonymous

When I think of someone with passion, purpose, and potential, I think of my favorite coach, Dick Vermeil, former head coach of XXXIV Super Bowl Champions St. Louis Rams. I love Coach Vermeil's authenticity. His passion oozes out. He doesn't apologize for it. It's who he is and we all loved it at Rams Park.

I remember during the "Greatest Show on Turf,"1999 regular season, Coach Vermeil could not hide his passion. He became emotional about his players and winning games. He cried. And it was contagious. That year felt magical. The starting quarterback went down with an injury; and God raised up a superstar, the new quarterback, Kurt Warner, a former grocery-store stocker. Everyone in business operations felt the passion, purpose, and potential of the entire coaching staff and the players. The season ended like a Cinderella story: Kurt Warner led the St. Louis Rams to a Super Bowl win.

So what is the difference between passion and purpose? Merriam-Webster.com defines passion as having zeal, excitement, or enthusiasm for something specific or about doing something specific. The Forbes website defines passion as putting more effort into something than is necessary (Geller 2013). Blogger Robert Chen says that when he learned the original meaning of the word "passion," as something we are willing to suffer for someone or something we love, he related it to the example of Jesus Christ. Chen said it changed his life, so much so that he no longer uses the word "passion" to describe something that he feels strongly about or that excites him. Instead, he uses the word to describe an activity, goal, or cause that he cares about so much that he's willing to suffer for it. He says this new ideal makes it easier for him to distinguish between something that is truly his "passion or simply a strong interest."

As I write this book, reading and learning about the different philosophies of authors and writers, such as Chen and others, has been an interesting experience. While I accept all these definitions of the word "passion," for purposes of this chapter, I will define it based on Merriam-Webster's definition, that is, having zeal, excitement or enthusiasm for something specific or about doing something specific. Now, that we have settled on a definition of passion, let's discuss the meaning of purpose.

I decided to write this chapter because I know many leaders, young and old, who are considering transitioning into a new career or new position within their companies. Many of us are looking for a new direction, searching for purpose in our lives, whether it's professionally, personally, or spiritually. I can personally speak to an exploration of this type from my own experiences.

Merriam-Webster's dictionary defines purpose as being intentional, having resolution and determination about something to be attained. An article published by The Greater Good Science Center at the University of California, Berkeley, says that, according to psychologists, purpose refers to the aim of achieving a long-term goal that is both personally meaningful and positive on a global scale.

When I think of purpose, I think of my "why." In other words, God's reason for my life. I believe God has given everyone a purpose in life, and it's up to us to manifest that God-given gift or purpose.

The two most important days in your life are the day you are born and the day you find out why.

—Mark Twain

I have heard some say that if we find our passion we will find our purpose. One of those individuals is Oprah Winfrey: "Follow your passion. It will lead you to your purpose." To some degree I believe that is true. I believe that passion is often confused with purpose. Passion relates to emotions, or the "what"; purpose relates to the reason, or the "why." Passion can change like the wind, but purpose generally lasts long-term. Passion can be selfish; it is inwardly focused. Passion is about what makes us feel good. Purpose is not a destination but a journey and practice. We don't find our purpose; we discover our purpose. The goals that foster a sense of purpose are goals that, potentially, can change lives. Purpose is about achieving something greater than ourselves. It's about making a positive impact on the world or others. I love the quote by an anonymous author that I started this chapter with: "Purpose is the reason you journey. Passion is the fire that lights your way. Potential is the skill needed to fulfill your purpose."

The miracle happens when we determine how to align our passion and purpose with our potential. I've been told that our purpose in life does not change over the years—like DNA. Now, I believe that to a certain extent. First of all, I did not know or even think about my purpose in life in my twenties. In those years, I concerned myself with my passions—emotional things that made me feel happy and enthusiastic. I did not think about what really mattered, what was possible, or why I did the things I did. I wasn't concerned with making an impact in the world or the lives of others. At least I was not intentional about it. I'm sure I did good for a lot of people, but I didn't equate that with my purpose in life.

Helping others has always made me happy. Growing up in church, I always believed the Bible verse, "From everyone who has been given much, much will be demanded," Luke 12:48 (NIV). My pastor has taught that our gifts are not meant to be kept to ourselves; instead, we are to share our gifts to benefit others. Now that I understand this concept, when I look back at what I thought was my purpose in life in my thirties, I must admit it's very close, if not the same as to what I believe today at age sixty. When I started reading and studying "purpose," I was not surprised to learn that I've known my purpose my entire life; that is, to benefit others as much as it was to benefit myself. That's what I've always believed in my life, even as the young and wiser Adrian, and I have shared this purpose through my volunteer work. I mean really, what's the purpose of having a gift and keeping it to yourself?

The meaning of life is to find your gift.
The purpose of life is to give it away.

—Pablo Picasso

We have discussed passion and purpose. Now let's talk about potential. Miriam-Webster.com defines potential as something having the possibility of achievement. Potential is critical in achieving our purpose, personally or organizationally. Without potential to accomplish our purpose, we will have a long road ahead of us.

Michael Jordan was, undoubtedly, one of the best—if not the best—National Basketball Association (NBA) player in the world. In 1993, Michael decided to retire from the NBA. In 1994, he pursued a new career in major league baseball. He only lasted about a year and never made it higher than AA ball, that is, the minor leagues. He batted .202 and finished with eleven fielding errors. In 1995, Michael returned to the Chicago Bulls basketball team and ended up winning three more NBA titles. Evidently, Michael Jordan had a passion for the game of baseball. Unfortunately, having passion is not enough to fulfill our purpose in life or business; we must have passion and potential. Michael Jordan excelled in basketball because he had passion and the potential that allowed him to fulfill his purpose. I'm not saying Michael Jordan could not have been an exceptional baseball player. I'm saying that it may have taken him longer to achieve the same success he did in basketball because basketball aligned with his strengths. Operating in our strengths allows us to discover our purpose.

When I graduated from high school, I wanted to be a lawyer because I believed it to be a prestigious career. I had watched *Perry Mason* on TV and thought that's what I wanted to do when I grew up. I believed I could help people who had been falsely accused to get out of trouble. In addition, I thought lawyers made a lot of money. I wanted money and a comfortable lifestyle for me and my family. It was my freshman year of college when my counselor told me she had read my transcript and SAT scores and thought I should take an accounting course. I explained to her that I wanted to be a lawyer. First of all, I had no idea what accounting was and was not aware of a career in accounting, nor what "CPA" (Certified Public Accountant) stood for. But I took the advice of my counselor. I relied on her strengths and took an accounting course in my freshman year. Surprisingly to me, I got an A. However, it wasn't a surprise to my counselor. She later told me that she saw my strengths in numbers and reasoning which is why she suggested the accounting course.

The good thing about accountants is we do not have to be geniuses in math, but we do need to be good with analytical and theoretical reasoning—which worked well for me. After taking the one course in accounting, I was hooked. I later graduated with my degree in accounting and went on to take and pass the CPA exam—by then I knew what it stood for. I probably would have been a good attorney, but I would have had to work harder because it wasn't aligned with my strengths, as with accounting. If we want to reach our dreams and discover our purpose in life, we must make sure the dreams are aligned with our strengths, passion, and potential. As it's been said, "If you do what you love, you'll never work a day in your life."

I loved accounting. I learned in college that an accountant's responsibility was to safeguard a company's assets. That knowledge gave me a sense of excitement knowing that I would be helping a company manage its money. I felt that accounting was the right career choice for me. It felt like my purpose. Discovering my purpose in life wasn't a topic of discussion at the dinner table in my family. For my family, having a job and making money was more important than anything—definitely more important than living a purpose-driven life.

So many of us wander through life without thinking about what matters, what is really important to us, or what is truly possible. It wasn't until I was in my late forties that I truly began to think about my "why" or my purpose in life. I remember reading Jeremiah 29:11: "'For I know the plans I have for you,' declares the Lord, 'plans to prosper you and not to harm you, plans to give you hope and a future'" (NIV). After reading that scripture, my curiosity began to pique as to why God put me on this earth. That was a halftime in my life.

At that time, I was working for the Arizona Cardinals as the CFO but felt unfulfilled. I felt like there was something more significant that I was called to do in life. Don't get me wrong. Working in the NFL was very significant, and I don't regret or take anything away from my experiences in the NFL. But I knew God had a calling for my life, and I was ready to discover the calling or purpose.

During that halftime, I took a course called "Writing Your Personal Mission Statement," offered by Stephen Covey and based on his book, *First Things First* (2003). It was at that time I realized my purpose in life. Ironically, my purpose, my "calling," was not something I found; it was something I discovered. It had always been there within me. As I mentioned before, it was something I had been doing all my life and something I had always been passionate about. It was something that came naturally for me and was aligned with my strengths, potential, and values. Like my DNA, it hadn't changed—and has not to this day.

During the Covey course, I wrote my personal mission statement: "Inspiring and enhancing the lives of women and girls." I have lived this purpose since my twenties; I just had not realized it was my calling. And I had not written it down. I have mentored women and girls my whole life. It is something I love to do and something that makes me feel like I am making a difference in the lives of others.

When I look back, I can see that it all started when, in my twenties, I learned that my niece, who was in the twelfth grade at the time, had decided not to continue school. I did not learn about this until I made a surprise visit to her school one day. The principal told me that my niece had missed forty-five days and that she would be expelled if she missed one more. Learning this, I immediately went to my sister's house and met with my niece, who had been sleeping. I packed her suitcase and she moved in with me. As you can imagine, she never missed another day from school and graduated from high school on time! On her graduation day, I made a vow to myself that I would make it my goal in life to continue to help women and girls reach their fullest potential.

When I look back at my career, I realize I did not fulfill my purpose in my day job, but I worked with women and girls by serving on boards of nonprofits. I served on the board of Greater St. Louis Girls, Incorporated for ten years. In addition,

I was on the board of directors for YWCA Metro St. Louis for three years, 1997-1999. By serving on these boards, I was able to utilize my talents and help inspire women and girls to live their best lives. During my tenure on the board of YWCA, I had no idea that I would, one day, become the CEO of the organization. I remember reading a quote by Gabrielle Bernstein, author, *You Are the Guru: 6 Messages to Help You Move Through Difficult Times with Certainty and Faith* (2020), that applied to my career: "Allow your passion to become your purpose, and it will one day become your profession."

When I was contacted to apply for the CEO position of YWCA, I was terrified. After all, at the time I was working as a CPA for an NFL team. What did I know about running a thirty-million-dollar nonprofit? I feared I did not have the potential or skills to be CEO of a company, a nonprofit at that. Then I remembered one of my favorite sayings; that is, we are not afraid of our failure, we are afraid of success, we are afraid of stepping out into our greatness. I have found that concept to be true in my case and in the case of many that I mentor and coach.

In my early years, I felt that my humble beginnings defined my destiny. Growing up in one of Miami's roughest and poorest neighborhoods, Liberty City, I believed, would hinder my success in life. I was young and thought, *Who am I to be smart, educated, brilliant, beautiful*...and so on. Then I remembered what the Bible said about me and I asked myself, *Why not me?*

I am fearfully and wonderfully made.

—Psalm 139:14 (NIV)

You are a chosen people, a royal priesthood,
a holy nation, God's special possession.

—1 Peter 2:9 (NIV)

Remembering those scriptures, I knew I had the potential and skills to be the CEO of not only YWCA but any organization God ordained for my life. That mindset didn't happen overnight. It took many years for me to develop a positive mental attitude (PMA).

When my husband and I were first dating, I thought the PMA messages he had hung around this office and house were from some kind of cult. I mean, I was not accustomed to repeating positive affirmations about myself or anyone else. The only affirmations I quoted at the time were from the Bible. However, the more I began to repeat and practice the positive affirmations, the more comfortable and confident I began to feel. In fact, one of the affirmations that stuck with me was by Napoleon Hill, author of *Think and Grow Rich* (1937): "Whatever the mind of man can conceive and believe, it can achieve." It reminded me of several Bible verses I had repeated in my life, which resulted in positive results of my belief materializing before me.

Besides passion, purpose, and potential, most organizations have a mission statement and vision statement. Of course, the values of the organization must support both statements. There are many explanations of a mission statement. Some say that a mission and purpose statement are the same; others beg to differ. The definition I use says a mission statement is a brief and concise statement of why an organization exists. Once a mission statement is written and accepted, I've learned as CEO of a nonprofit, it's important not to mission creep—which means to make a gradual shift in the original goals of the organization. Mission creep may not be negative unless the shift prevents the organization from fulfilling its mission. For example, the mission of an organization may be to provide housing for homeless women, but let's say there comes an abundance of funding through a federal grant for animal relief. The agency decides to apply for the animal-relief funding just because the money is available. Hence, mission creep because the animal-relief funding deviates from the organization's original vision, mission, and purpose. However, there are circumstances where an organization may shift from its original mission, which is typically a well-thought-out strategic decision. An example would be an acquisition or merger which expands the services of the organization.

I dream, I test my dreams against my beliefs, I dare to take risks, and I execute my vision to make those dreams come true.

—Walt Disney

According to Wikipedia contributors (2021), a vision statement reflects an idealistic emotional vision of an organization or group's future. Microsoft's corporate vision statement is "To help people and businesses throughout the world realize their full potential" (Gregory 2016). I believe it would be difficult for a company or individual to achieve their purpose in life without a vision. Helen Keller, author, lecture, and activist, said, "The only thing worse than being blind is having sight and no vision."

When I think of most, if not all, successful athletes and businesspeople, one thing they have in common is a vision. They create a mental picture of the result they want to achieve, then they do everything in their power to make it happen. The vision is clear, powerful, and so big it takes them out of their comfort zone.

When Coach Vermeil became head coach of the St. Louis Rams in 1997, he had the vision to win a Super Bowl. Through building the right team, hard work, and strategic planning, Coach Vermeil's vision came to fruition in February 2000 by winning Super Bowl XXXIV.

As I write this chapter today, it is January 1, 2021. Most, if not all Americans, would say good riddance to 2020! A year of pain, loss, and suffering for so many people across the globe due to the pandemic. As I look ahead to the future, I ask myself, *Did 2020 change my perspective in life? Did my passion, purpose, potential, mission, or vision change?* The answer is "partially." The one constant that did not change is my purpose. I was born to inspire and enhance the lives of women and girls. My passion, on the other hand, has expanded. Due to the racial injustices in 2020, my passion has grown to include fighting for racial equity for people of color—and I mean including but not limited to income, education, housing, and healthcare. Racial equity is when race does not determine the socioeconomic outcomes of a person and when justice is for all Americans, especially people of color. This expanded passion does not take away from my passion to help women live their best lives; it adds to it.

Pay attention to the things you are naturally drawn to. They are often, connected to your path passion, and purpose in life. Have the courage to follow them.

—Ruben Chavez, creator of @thinkgrowprosper

To wrap up this chapter on the three Ps—purpose, passion, and potential—I reiterate the importance of potential in achieving our purpose in life. One last example of this came to me in my childhood. Growing up in my neighborhood, all the boys wanted to be athletes, primarily football players. For some boys that became a reality, but for the majority it was an unrealistic dream. You see, they simply did not have the potential or skills to achieve what they thought was their purpose in life, to be a football player. It is only when our passion and purpose align with our potential that we can do anything we put our minds to.

When you catch a glimpse of your potential,
that's when passion is born.
—Zig Ziglar, *Born to Win: Find Your Success Code*

My mission in life has always been to inspire and enhance the lives of women and girls. Since retiring from the YWCA on June 30, 2021, I have expanded that mission to include helping women leaders embrace the greatness within as they inspire others to do the same; my broadened vision is "All women will achieve their fullest potential." In conjunction with the mission and vision statement, I want us to remember values, professionally or personally. Values are characteristics, beliefs, principles, and behaviors that drive personal and business decisions. As I stated earlier, values should be aligned with our passion and purpose.

Success is knowing your purpose in life, growing to reach your maximum potential, and sowing seeds that benefit others.
—John C. Maxwell, *Developing the Leader Within You*

Chapter Seven:

Having a Winner's Mindset

Winners are not those who never fail,
but those who never quit.
—Edwin Louis Cole, founder Christian Men's Network

When I think of having a winner's mindset, I think of my days as vice president of finance for the St. Louis Rams. In 1997, when Coach Dick Vermeil became head coach of the Rams, we had a losing record of 5-11. The following year, in 1998, instead of improving, the record worsened, finishing 4-12. People called the St. Louis Rams the "St. Louis Lambs." It looked dismal to say the least. But in 1999, the St. Louis Rams shocked the nation and finished the regular season with a record of 13-3. They went on to defeat the Tennessee Titans in Super Bowl XXXIV on January 30, 2000.

Coach Vermeil was a great leader as head coach for the Rams. He possessed all the characteristics of a winner's mindset: confidence, persistence, resilience, to name a few. A good leader must be able to motivate and support each team member. Coach Vermeil and the coaching staff did just that. They were able to determine the team's weaknesses and maximize each player's strengths. After that, it was up to the individual player to develop a winner's mindset, perform at his best, and hold his teammates accountable to do the same. As a result, the former St. Louis Rams, now the Los Angeles Rams, carry the title of Super Bowl Champions.

As I was writing this book, January 2021, I happened to be watching the television show *60 Minutes* and saw a story that motivated me to write about it. It was about a football player who had made a remarkable comeback from a diagnosed career-ending injury. His name is Alex Smith.

Smith was 2005's NFL number-one overall draft pick. In 2018, as quarterback for Washington (formerly Redskins), he suffered a compound-fracture injury to his right leg which led to a life-threatening sepsis and necrotizing fasciitis that required seventeen surgeries to prevent amputation. The severity of his injury did not keep Smith from believing he would, one day, recover.

After a lengthy rehabilitation process, Smith returned to football in 2020 as a reserve quarterback for Washington. Midway through the season, he was named starting quarterback. Smith ended that season with a 5-1 record and led his team to an NFC East division title game.

In the *60 Minutes* interview, Smith talked in detail about his journey. The doctor who appeared with him shared how he saw a fight in Smith's eyes when told he may have to have his leg amputated. Alex Smith's story exemplifies the heart and mind of a winner.

Winners never quit and quitters never win.

—Vince Lombardi, late head coach

How do you define a winner's mindset? I've seen several definitions. One definition I like to use is having the courage and fortitude to not give up or lose your motivation after failure or adversity. When I think of successful businesspeople and athletes, I think of determination, grit, and resilience. Let's be clear. Having a winner's mindset doesn't necessarily mean that you will always win. Remember, we may fail even with a winner's mindset, but we must never give up.

For me, having a winner's mindset starts with faith. Faith is the foundation of how I think of myself, how I create my values and my beliefs. When I'm grounded in my faith, I have the confidence to overcome adversity and failure. Faith helps me to have the positive mental attitude that I need when self-doubt creeps in; it helps me to see myself as a winner even when I don't feel that way and things look grim.

> *If you don't see yourself as a winner,*
> *then you cannot perform as a winner.*
> —Zig Ziglar, *Born to Win: Find Your Success Code*

A winner's mindset carries several traits:

Clear goals. Know what you want to achieve and where you want to go, then you have a chance of reaching your destination.

Self-awareness. Be conscious of your feelings, motives, thoughts, habits, character, and behavior.

Confidence. Trust and believe in your own abilities.

Resilience. Be able to recover from failure, adversity, or difficult life events.

Other traits include self-discipline, perseverance, optimism...the list goes on. All of the traits are important in developing a winner's mindset, but I believe that setting **clear**

goals is one of the first steps. After all, how can we win if we don't know what we're trying to win.

When I took over as CEO of YWCA Metro St. Louis, I had a goal of improving the agency's financial stability. I knew what I wanted to achieve and I knew it would not be easy, but I was determined and confident that it would happen. I developed and focused on my game plan. It took nearly two years, but I accomplished my goal by having a winner's mindset.

Developing a winner's mindset also requires **self-awareness**. This is a trait I have practiced over the years. For me **self-awareness** includes knowing what I want in life and focusing on that outcome.

We have heard sayings like, "What we focus on becomes real" or "What we focus on we attract." Let me share a story with you.

My husband and I decided to have our first outside lunch during the pandemic. I was on vacation that day, so I decided to wear my new dress and cute wedge high-heeled shoes. I loved those shoes, not only because they cost me $150 but they were comfortable—just dangerous for me to walk in. But I wanted to look cute for my husband on our first lunch date in months.

After lunch we were walking back to the car. Straight ahead I saw a rock and said to myself, *Do not walk on the rock because you may fall.* I've had experience in this area; I knew what my mind was telling me. So I began to focus on the rock. I began to visualize what would happen if I stepped the wrong way on this rock. The thought began to feel real and I was fixated on not falling. As we got closer, I took my eyes off the rock to look at something in the distance. Before I knew it, I walked on the rock and twisted my foot. Later at the urgent care, I was told it was broken. What happened? I focused on what I did not want, instead of what I wanted. That became my reality. (Needless to say, my husband threw my favorite shoes in the garbage after we returned home. This was the second trip to urgent care because of those shoes. The first time was a sprained toe. That's another story for another time!)

Speaking of my husband, Vito has a winner's mindset. In fact, you would think he was born with it. He exudes **confidence**, **resilience**, and so on. He's an athlete, and I have always admired his positive mental attitude. Me, on the other hand, I had to develop a winner's mindset. I had run track in high school and had the **confidence** and mindset needed to be a winner on the track. However, for many of my professional years, I struggled with self-**confidence**. It's hard, if not impossible, to have a winner's mindset with a lack of self-**confidence**.

Some women and girls lack self-**confidence**. It is not uncommon. Throughout my life, I struggled with building self-**confidence** and a winner's mindset. It was not easy for me. It was also sometimes uncomfortable. When I was in high school, I participated in a scholarship essay competition. Out of ten students, eight were girls. Out of the eight girls, one hundred percent said they lacked **confidence** and wanted to improve on it. Good news: Self-**confidence** can be developed. And it's something I will never regret developing.

Your success will be determined by your own confidence and fortitude.

—Michelle Obama, *Becoming*

When I am asked for one word to describe myself, I typically say "resilient." Resiliency has been a dominant theme in my life story, personally and professionally. Since the age of thirteen, I cannot remember one year in my life that I did not have to rely on **resilience**.

As you can imagine, achieving a successful career after being given away by my biological, mentally ill mother and then being adopted at age ten was no small feat. I was resilient then. I clearly see **resilience** as I think back to my high school track days and not always winning. I stood up after each defeat. Resilient people and teams bounce back from adversities. What's amazing to me is that after living through hard times and lacking self-**confidence**, I still excelled in my life and career. My inner self, the real self, always believed I would succeed no matter what. Giving up was not an option. That's **resilience**; that's a winner's mindset.

I remember in high school running the 400-meter relay. The only thing on my mind was being the fastest to cross the finish line. Speed is one key ingredient to winning a race, but there are other factors involved, too, such as being well-coordinated and having the ability to pass the baton to the next runner at maximum speed without dropping it. As I watched the 2020 track and field Olympics in Tokyo, I was nervous. Team USA had performed poorly in the early races due to poor passing of the baton. Fortunately, they came out on top on the last day of the track and field competition in the 4x400-meters relay. Speed, coordination, and the ability to pass the baton were the key ingredients for Team USA. But let's not forget it started with having a winner's mindset.

In 2018, as CEO for YWCA Metro St. Louis, I was at another halftime in my life. It was during that halftime I made a decision. It was time to pass the baton to someone else and move into my next career chapter: executive and leadership coach for businesswomen and public speaker.

Being CEO for over a decade had been a fulling journey, but it was time for something new. I had planned to make my career transition in 2020. Unfortunately, during that year, the pandemic brought on new challenges for businesses and career transitions. I decided to wait until the environment stabilized before making my move. Now, today, in 2021, with the pandemic abating somewhat, I am making the transition from serving as CEO of YWCA Metro St. Louis to owning my own company. Having a winner's mindset has helped me to plan this leap of faith.

I talked earlier about the importance of having a positive mental attitude in winning, whether personally or professionally. I believe that having a winner's mindset starts with our thinking.

I remember reading what Paul said to the people of Philippi, "...whatever is true, whatever is noble, whatever is right, whatever is pure, whatever is lovely, whatever is admirable—if anything is excellent or praiseworthy—think about such things," Philippians 4:8 (NIV). Then Paul said, "I can do all things through Him who gives me strength," Philippians 4:13 (NIV). Those quotations lead me to believing that winning starts in my mind, in what I think and believe.

> *Winners win in life because they*
> *win the battle in their mind first!*
>
> —Tony Gaskins, *The Dream Chaser*

Since the age of fifteen and working for Burger King, I have never been without a job. Before retiring from YWCA, I'd worked for someone else for over forty-five years, nonstop. I had never dreamed of being an entrepreneur. So to prepare myself for the 2021 upcoming chapter in my career, I hired a branding coach. I knew I needed an expert to help me with this major transition in my life.

I researched the web and found many coaches and consultants experienced in helping individuals and businesses create their brands. I was fortunate to find someone right in my backyard, Lethia Owens, founder of Game Changers International. Hiring Lethia was one of the best investments I could have made. I made another big investment when I hired my executive coach, Edie, in 2020. These two valuable coaches remind me of a Bible verse I love: "Plans fail for lack of counsel, but with many advisers they succeed," Proverbs 15:22 (NIV). Without good counsel from Edie, Lethia, and my husband, Vito, I would not be writing this book today or starting my own business. Having experienced people to help us succeed is important. In my early career, my boss would tell me, "Adrian, if you're the smartest person in the room, the room is too small." Since then, I've always surrounded myself with people who could help guide me along the way so that I could then turn around and do the same for others needing my guidance.

As I began to develop a strategic plan for my next career journey after the YWCA, I knew I wanted to be an executive coach. It's in line with my purpose, or calling, in life of inspiring and enhancing the lives of women and girls. In addition, it's something that comes easily. I have a passion for helping women. Executive coaching falls within my wheelhouse. But I needed help getting started, which is why I hired Lethia.

I attended Lethia's weekend workshop on "Brand Your Brilliance" with four dynamic women. Lethia led us through the weekend's objectives, where she and her team guided the participants through an amazing experience. One of the greatest of which for me resulted in the creation of my signature system, "EmBrace."

Working with my clients through the process of my signature system, I help them to transform, grow, stretch, or shift. I selected the word "EmBrace" to represent my system, which speaks to my mission of helping women leaders and aspiring women leaders embrace the greatness within, as they inspire others to do the same.

To embrace the greatness within doesn't always come easily for women. It didn't for me. I wish I had had a system or coach to help me discover my greatness a long time ago. But it took years for me to accept, willingly and enthusiastically, the greatness that God has given me to share with the world.

My signature system, EmBrace:

E = Empowerment. Empower yourself to be great.

M = Movement. Take action.

B = Belief. Believe in yourself.

R = Resilience. Never give up.

A = Accountability. Be accountable to yourself and others.

C = Courage. Step out on faith.

E = Evaluate. Monitor and evaluate your progress regularly.

Embrace who you are and your divine purpose.
Identify the barriers in your life, and develop
discipline, courage, and the strength to permanently
move beyond them, and keep moving forward.

—Germany Kent, media personality, businesswoman,
model, actress, philanthropist

(E)=Empowerment means finding the strength and the confidence to take control over our lives and not giving away our power. The winner's mindset begins with empowering ourselves to be great.

I spent years worrying about what other people thought of me and wanting their approval. I felt that I had to have more than the next person in order to be considered successful. For example, obtaining my CPA and MBA. This belief stemmed from growing up Black in the sixties and seventies in the south. I know most people don't consider Miami, Florida, "the south" these days, but in the sixties and seventies, for me, it was the deep south. The only women role-models I had were my grandmother, a housekeeper for a Jewish family, and my adoptive mom, Dorothy, at the time a housewife. Mom eventually got a job as a social worker when I was in the tenth grade. She had never graduated from college, but I remember how proud I was of her for getting a job that she loved and embraced. As a social worker, she helped the elderly find resources, such as Medicaid supplements, art classes, and educational trainings to name a few. She taught me the meaning of self-empowerment. It took me a while, but Mom helped me realize my personal values and self-worth were key to discovering the greatness within me.

(M)=Movement means to take action, to do something that influences advancement toward a certain direction, decision, or goal. A winner's mindset results when we take action.

As a leader, I remember an encounter when one of my team members was frustrated with me because I would not make a decision to approve a certain policy. I was hesitant because the new policy dealt with a major HR change to employees' personal time off (PTO). You know the saying, "It's been done this way forever, so why change?" That's the feedback I received from some employees. The policy was more beneficial to the employee than to the employer, but I knew deep down inside I needed to approve the policy change for the good of the company. However, making a decision is not enough; we must act on the decision. So I told my team member I needed more time, even though I had had the policy to review for over a week. I wanted to make sure things were perfect, and I did not want to overlook something important.

After a week, she said to me, "Please, just make a decision. Whether it's right or wrong, we just need a decision." In other words, she was asking me to take action...to move forward. After long consideration of the impact this decision would have on employee morale, I decided to approve the change in the PTO policy. That was a tough decision.

Back then, I didn't realize one of the reasons for my hesitation to take action, but today I do. As I said before, I am a recovering perfectionist, and I would hold up making decisions until I thought everything was right. But what I've learned over the years is that waiting for everything to be perfect does not work. There will always be something that is not exactly perfect and could definitely be better. There is no perfect time. We only have the present time. We must take action and move toward our goals. We can always make adjustments and pivot if needed, and if we can't make adjustments or pivot, as leaders, we have to accept the consequences.

That's what I had to tell myself as I started writing this book. I made the decision three years ago to write it, but I did not put that decision into action until my coach, Edie, challenged me in the fall of 2020. Winner's love a good challenge!

The other area that kept me from moving forward on making decisions: I overthought everything. I obsessed over every detail. Paralysis of analysis stifled me, so it took me forever to move or take action. I realized part of my issue was my accounting career and the need to make sure everything was black and white—to leave no room for gray. This is where building confidence and believing in yourself comes into play.

The best time to plant a tree was 20 years ago.
The second-best time is now.

—Chinese Proverb

(B)=Belief is the third step in my signature system to developing a winner's mindset—and one of the most critical steps. I believe that winning starts in the mind by developing our thoughts; then those thoughts become our words and the words become our actions. As I've mentioned several times in this book, my faith is the foundation of my beliefs in who I am. If I find myself believing disempowerment thoughts, I stop and remember, I can do all things through Him who gives me strength. I remind myself that my destiny lies within me through the power of my faith.

Believing in yourself means having confidence in your ability to achieve what you set your mind to do. Self-belief develops self-worth and self-love. Believing in yourself has more benefits than just achieving your goals, such as living a life of happiness and well-being.

Past experiences can lead to self-doubt and unbelief in ourselves. Those past experiences can include a poor performance review on the job or not getting promoted when you felt you deserved it. These experiences can easily take away your confidence and power. Developing a mindset of self-belief allows you to take back your power. To live a life of full potential, we must fully believe in our abilities to accomplish our goals.

I am the greatest, I said that even before I knew I was.

—Muhammad Ali

(R)=Resilience allows us to recover from failure, adversity, or difficult life events. I shared a story about my resilience earlier in this chapter, and we will talk more about resilience in chapter nine. I believe having resilience as a leader is so important that I've dedicated an entire chapter on it. When I think of resilience today, August 2021, a week after the Olympics, I think of Simone Biles, an American artistic gymnast, and other athletes who were vulnerable enough to share with the world their mental struggles. It took resilience for Biles to bounce back from what we now know as the "twisties," that is, when gymnasts lose awareness of their routine while in the air.

I have had many personal and professional events in my life where my resilience bubbled up from within. I remember times in my career when I did not think I would survive an untrue accusation by an employee or racial and gender injustice directed at me. I've had to overcome some serious hurdles in my personal and professional life. I have the battle scars to show the adversities that helped me develop a winner's mindset. But it all made me a stronger person. Maybe that will be another book!

(A)=Accountability means taking responsibility for something we have done or promised we would do. For me, accountability and integrity go hand in hand. As a former accountant for over twenty-five years, being accountable

is a given. It's in my DNA. I remember talking about team accountability with a former colleague who played football for the Rams. He told me that if you want to reach the optimal achievement in the game—which is winning—every teammate must be held accountable to one's self and each other. It's a two-way street. Accountability is another important ingredient in my EmBrace signature system, so important, in fact, that, like resilience, I devoted an entire chapter on this topic. We will discuss accountability further in chapter eight.

Accountability is the glue that ties commitment to the result.

—Bob Proctor, *Change Your Paradigm, Change Your Life*

(C)=Courage to me is a choice to face and confront adversity, pain, or danger despite the fear or opposition. Having a winner's mindset requires courage, a character trait that is vital for all leaders to possess. In my younger days, I believed we were either born with courage or not. I also felt the same way about confidence. It wasn't until I got older that I learned that having courage and confidence is a choice. It took courage for me to leave a promising career with the Miami Dolphins in 1995 to move to a city I knew little or nothing about, St. Louis. I moved to St. Louis on faith and prayer. God sent me two wonderful ladies, Angela and Anne-Marie who were my very first friends in St. Louis. Today twenty-six years later, we are still good friends.

Courage is being comfortable with not knowing the outcome of your situation. That's not easy for most people. I've always been the type of person that wants to know the outcome before I make a decision. Having the courage to retire in 2021 without knowing what lies ahead was easier for me than moving to St. Louis in 1995. You see, I've grown in my faith over the years. I've developed more confidence, perseverance, stamina, mental strength, and boldness. For me courage is like a muscle, that I continually develop every day.

(E)=Evaluate can be defined in many ways. For me, "evaluate" means to determine and assess the effectiveness of an action that I have performed or a decision that I have chosen. I use both "action" and "decision" in my definition because simply making a decision does not constitute action. As leaders, there are times we want to evaluate, analyze, or consider our decisions or thought processes before we take action. We may want to weigh the cost and risk of the outcome we wish to achieve, which is critical for major decisions. As my coach, Edie, says in a recent email:

Evaluating is the deliberate feedback loop for all champions on the continuous-improvement track. World-class champions practice deliberately and evaluate their progress regularly in an effort to link the winning mindset to a winning outcome or result. Practice is the natural training system in business or sports and evaluation is the metric for assessing the effectiveness of action.

We've all heard the saying, "Experience is the best teacher," right? John Maxwell argues and says, "Experience is not the best teacher; *evaluated* experience is the best teacher" (2011). Evaluated experience is how we determine if there is a need to pivot or if we are on the right path. It's our learning curve to success.

In summary, having a winner's mindset is knowing what we want, setting goals to achieve what we want, not giving up, believing in ourselves, and knowing that winning is a journey, not a destination.

And remember, EmBrace the greatness within so you can inspire others to do the same!

Chapter Eight:
Accountability – No Excuses

Accountability breeds response-ability.

—Stephen R. Covey, *The 7 Habits of Highly Effective People*

As I said before, accountability means taking responsibility for something we have done or promised we would do. It does not mean trying to catch an employee doing something wrong; it means being willing to accept or account for our own actions. The importance of accountability can be seen at many levels in good leadership. One main reason for its importance—whether in sports, business, or our personal lives—is that accountability builds *trust* in relationships. And trust builds winning teams.

Accountability builds trust within a team. When our teammates, whether on the field or in the office, can trust us to do our job at a level of excellence and go above our job description for the benefit of the team, we will earn a reputation that can accelerate our career and build valuable relationships. Every winning team must have trust to achieve their ultimate goal. In football, that's winning the Super Bowl. The team that wins the Super Bowl is the NFL's *champion*. To win this ultimate prize, the team must first make it to the big game. No easy task, as you can imagine, but it couldn't be done if the trust did not exist within the team.

An NFL season consists of sixteen games currently, and you would think that the team with the most wins automatically becomes the champs. Usually, the team entering the Super Bowl with the most games won for the regular season is considered the favored team to win the big game. But the New York Giants proved that to be wrong. In 2008, during my tenure as CFO for the Arizona Cardinals, my husband, Vito, and I had the privilege of having front row seats at Super Bowl XLII in the University of Phoenix Stadium—a game remembered as one of the greatest games ever played. The New England Patriots were playing against the New York Giants. New England had ended the 2007 regular season with a 16-0 record, one of the first teams since the 1972 Miami Dolphins to end a regular season undefeated. The New York Giants, on the other hand, ended the season that year with a 10-6 record. You would think the Giants would be the underdog then, right? Wrong. They made history by becoming the first NFC wild-card team to win a Super Bowl. So how did they win? Accountability.

As a team, players are accountable not only to themselves but also to their teammates. As I said, accountability means taking responsibility for what we have promised. Players promise and commit to their coaches and to their teammates that that they will perform to the best of their ability. Each member of the New York Giants on that day in 2008 was accountable to their coach, to each other, and to the game. And that accountability created a winning team!

On good teams coaches hold players accountable,
on great teams players hold players accountable.
—Joe Dumars, chief strategy officer, Sacramento Kings;
former professional basketball player

Let's take a look at the difference between accountability and responsibility.

When a manager hires an employee or a football team signs a player, there is a job description. The job description should be clear and outline the responsibilities and expectations of the position. The supervisor can measure the performance of those responsibilities and expectations because it's in the job description. Let's say a leader hires an assistant to handle the mail and answer the telephone. If the new hire handles both responsibilities correctly, he will get a good performance review. Let's try this scenario though: Say for two days the telephone did not ring the entire time, which was highly unusual for the business. After two days, the new-hire's boss discovered the telephone system was out of order. When asked why he did not report the telephones were not ringing, the employee said, "It's not in my job description to detect if the telephone system is working or not. I was hired to answer the telephone when it rings." True. Detecting a problem was not in the employee's job description. According to the job description, the employee had an obligation only to *answer* the telephone.

Being accountable to a team goes beyond personal responsibility or the words of a job description. Accountability takes into account the outcome for the entire team or company. Let's say that organization was a call center for women fleeing from sexual assault or domestic violence. Two days of no calls could have been a life-or-death situation for a woman. An accountable employee would have notified their boss after an hour or two of no calls.

You can see that responsibility is measurable because it's clearly defined in a job description; it's an obligation for the employee to act. On the other hand, accountability is an obligation to answer for an action. We cannot force someone to be accountable; it is a choice. The employee in the above scenario had a choice whether or not to go beyond the job description and notify someone that the telephone was not ringing. He chose not to.

Leaders can hold an employee responsible for what can be measured, for what is defined in the job description. Leaders cannot make an employee accountable. The employee has to want it.

Being a part of a team demands a sense of accountability. When working on a team, we know that our teammates depend on us to go beyond our job description, when necessary, to benefit the entire team.

In another scenario, going back to football, imagine a defensive end, whose primary responsibility is to keep the opposing running back from gaining yardage. Imagine the ball falling right into the defensive end's hands. Now imagine that he is unaccountable to his team and decides to let the ball fall to the ground because catching the ball is not in his job description. Had the defensive end chosen to be accountable to his team, he would have held the catch for an interception.

Accountability in the workplace establishes and holds people to a common expectation by clearly defining the company's mission, values, and goals. That expectation means holding each employee responsible for achieving the company's goals identified in the company's strategic plan.

To create a culture of accountability, I believe it starts with the leader. Remember what Vito says, "Speed of the leader, speed of the team." Vito is one of the most accountable human beings I know. He is a man of his word and he expects the same from others. Unfortunately, I have to constantly remind him that everyone in the world is not as accountable as he is. Being accountable is not easy for everyone. It may sound simple, but creating a life of accountability starts with having the right mindset.

Being an accountable leader is having a mindset that we are willing to keep our commitment to our team, no matter the adversity or challenges that we face, unless it is detrimental to one's mental health, as in the case of Simone Biles. Accountability is a choice and a mindset, not a skill. That is good news for organizations that want to develop accountable leaders. Developing a culture of accountable leaders includes, but is not limited to 1) hiring the right people; 2) setting clear expectations; 3) communicating with authenticity and transparency; 4) addressing conflict or concerns right away; 5) building trust; 6) delegating authority; and 7) celebrating milestones and successes. Once companies develop accountable leaders, they are on their way to developing an organization committed to accountability.

A company's mission, values, and goals are critical in setting the course for the business at hand. Likewise, and of equal importance, a leader's personal mission statement, values, and goals set the course for leadership and should align with the company's mission, values, and goals.

The mission of YWCA, nationally, is to "eliminate racism and empower women." Currently, YWCA Metro St. Louis states their values as collaboration, compassion, excellence, integrity, intelligence, and respect—which aligns with YWCA nationally. In turn, my personal mission statement, as I stated in an earlier chapter, is to inspire and enhance the lives of women and girls, which aligns with YWCA's mission. My personal values of accountability, empathy, excellence, integrity, and respect also align with YWCA's values.

There are many reasons why personal mission and values should align with the company's mission and values. I have narrowed my top three down to 1) employee retention, 2) increased productivity, and 3) a happier work environment.

Employee retention

I have experienced as a leader, especially in the nonprofit sector, that most employees are drawn to the agency because of its mission and values. They tend to stay with the agency even when the salary is not as competitive as the market if the mission and values align with their own. Employees love the work they do and tend to feel like they are working for a higher calling; they feel accountable to making sure they represent the agency well; they serve with pride, honor, and loyalty because they believe in the mission and values of the company.

When I first met my husband, he worked for a national insurance company. His loyalty to the company, because of its mission and values, impressed me. The mission and values hung prominently on the wall of his home office. I teased him and called the company a "cult." After we were married and I attended several of his company meetings with him, I understood his passion. Hundreds of employees filled each meeting and all cheered the company's mission and values. I had goose-bumps. I had never experienced a room full of passion and excitement by employees like that. The experience came close to a football game and the cheering crowd. But the football crowd does not cheer because of the team's mission and values; as you can imagine, it cheers for the team. My husband worked for that insurance company for over twenty-two years because his personal mission and values aligned with the company's mission and values.

A team aligned with the company's mission and values will create successful outcomes.

—Adrian E. Bracy

Increased productivity

Hiring a team that is aligned with the mission and values of the company is critical for company leaders to increase productivity. I have experienced this firsthand. In my corporate days, I experienced that even when disagreements or dysfunction revealed themselves within a team, if the team aligned with the values of the company, success ultimately prevailed. Think of it this way: It's impossible for a team of six to be rowing down a river in a canoe with all hands rowing in the same direction and end up in different locations. Okay. That was a trick scenario. First of all, they are in the same canoe, so it's impossible for them to end up in different locations, but you get the point. When a team is firing on all cylinders, increased productivity will result. In addition, team members will feel a sense of accountability to the team. Having clear and concise expectations is key to success for any team's productivity.

Happier work environment

A happier work environment emerges when the team aligns with the mission and values of the company. In 2019, I had the pleasure of attending a business meeting where Sam Silverstein, an accountability expert, presented. Before that meeting, I had not met Sam, but my marketing coach, Lethia Owens, spoke highly of him.

Sam's talk had so motivated me that after his presentation I waited to meet him personally and purchase a book or two. After the room emptied, I went over to Sam's table. I put my coffee cup down by his books to reach into my purse to get my money. As I pulled out my wallet, I knocked over my cup of coffee. With natural instinct, Sam grabbed the books and I pulled the tablecloth off the table. It was like magic. We worked as a team toward a common goal and were satisfied with the outcome. We laughed at how spontaneously we worked together to save the books. Not one book was ruined, and I ended up purchasing five books instead of one or two.

So that brings me to another reason why I believe personal and company alignment makes for a happier work environment. But first let me tell you a little bit more about Sam Silverstein. Sam is an author, speaker, and entrepreneur. He dedicates his life to empowering people to live accountable lives, transform the way they do business, and create a more accountable world.

Starting work on this chapter, I researched the word "accountability." It wasn't long after that I thought of Sam Silverstein. I pulled out one of the five books I had purchased and saved from my coffee spill. As I began to write this section, I remembered a story Sam told at that meeting about a bank in Amarillo, Texas, called "Happy State Bank." I thought it was, both, a fictitious name and story because it sounded too good to be true.

The book is titled *Non-Negotiable: The Story of Happy State Bank & The Power of Accountability* (2015); the foreword was written by J. Pat Hickman, chairman and CEO of Happy State Bank and Trust Co. I pulled the book out to skim the chapters to see if there was a quote I could use by Sam. Instead, I read practically the entire book in one sitting. I have to admit. I love buying books, but I don't always get to read them. When I hesitate to buy books, I always hear my husband's voice in my head, "It's better to have and not need than to need and not have." So I buy books just in case I need them one day. And having purchased Sam's book was a blessing because it allowed me to include some of his information in my book; i.e., the alignment of employee and company core values, accountability to each other and the mission of the organization, which all make for a happier work environment.

In Sam's book, he states:

The Power of Accountability is when you value people, know what you believe, what your mission is, what is in your control, and what is truly non-negotiable for you, and everyone on your team understands and lives by those non-negotiables, then you will create an environment where people can be their very best both for themselves and the organization. The natural outflow is a place where accountability is abundant and people keep their commitments to themselves and to others (Silverstein, 53-54).

I find every word in this statement to be true. Creating an accountable workplace starts with all leaders and employees valuing people, standing for what they believe in, and believing in the company mission. Because of the Happy Bank story, I became specifically fond of the idea of knowing what's in my control and what are my non-negotiables.

When hired, Happy State Bank's employees agree to honor the company's twenty non-negotiables. If they do not agree, their employment is on the line. Knowing their employees agree to these non-negotiables enables the leaders to know that they have alignment within the team with the values they seek to promote. This alignment between employees and the bank helped to produce one of the most financially sound banks in Texas during the 2008 financial downturn. In addition, low employee turnover at Happy Bank stems from employees feeling appreciated and valued. It makes for a happier work environment.

Accountable leaders don't make excuses. Instead, they understand that mistakes, failures, and setbacks are all learning opportunities. They don't play the blame game and throw others under the bus. They take ownership of the outcome and work to find solutions. Accountable leaders know how to turn lemons into lemonade. They think and say "we" instead of "I," which builds camaraderie, trust, and a responsible mindset within the team.

Accountability is a decision and a commitment that requires self-discipline. As it relates to accountability, self-discipline is having—and using—the ability to do what we should do even if we do not feel like it. When leaders practice self-discipline, they maintain focus despite the many distractions all around.

I believe achieving personal and professional goals relies on self-discipline. A quote by motivational speaker

Jim Rohn states, "Discipline is the bridge between goals and accomplishment." How does one remain self-disciplined when things get rough or when temptation all around urges one to give up? For me, it's my faith. Self-discipline requires having a strong desire to achieve a specific goal. That strong desire is driven by inspiration, motivation, and faith.

Motivation gets you going
but discipline keeps you growing.
—John C. Maxwell, *Developing the Leader Within You*

For the past twelve years, every January, I have practiced an annual spiritual tradition that requires self-discipline. When I depend on my own strength to accomplish the task, I fail every time; but when I depend on my faith, I am able to achieve my annual spiritual tradition without a hitch. There are days when, due to circumstances, I have difficulty staying focused on the many tasks requiring my attention. It takes self-discipline to avoid losing focus. To get my focus back, I stop and take five minutes to meditate. Meditation requires self-discipline and being intentional. The same is true for my professional life. Self-discipline in the workplace is much easier when I have a targeted goal that's important to me and brings value to me and others.

Accountable leaders do not depend on their feelings and emotions; they do what they have to do despite the circumstances. Accountability requires taking responsibility and ownership for outcomes that are expected of us. Make no mistake. This is not always easy to do, but it's necessary for success, professionally and personally. We can learn to be accountable leaders, but it requires us to be intentional. "Being intentional" means having the awareness of what we are doing, being deliberate and purposeful about our actions. It's one thing to be an accountable leader, but it's another thing to hold our team accountable. This is where most leaders struggle. When team members are not held accountable for poor performance, disruptive behavior, or missed deadlines, the credibility of the leader diminishes. Ultimately, the morale of the team suffers and the leader loses the chance to inspire the team to become high-performing.

There are times as leaders when we become desperate to hire someone because of a critical game or project. But if we are not intentional and we hire based on emotions, the result can backfire. Hiring a person that's not a good fit for the organization usually ends up in a negative impact on both parties. I have read of companies that offer employees a "quitting bonus" if they leave within the probation period. In the long-run, this can be a benefit to both the company and the employee.

The choices we make are
ultimately our own responsibility.

—Eleanor Roosevelt

Qualities of an accountable leader are numerous. Some of my favorites include:

Self-awareness. Leaders should know and understand themselves; that is, they need to be conscious of their feelings, motives, thoughts, habits, character, and behavior. It is written that self-awareness is one of the key elements to emotional intelligence. According to the Northern Arizona University website (https://events.nau.edu/event/ virtual-professional-development-emotional-intelligence-overview/), "emotional intelligence" is the ability to recognize our own emotions and those of others. You might have noticed that self-awareness enters into more than just an accountable leader; it is a trait of a resilient leader, helps overcome fear, and is part of the winner's mindset.

Trust and Integrity. The foundation of accountability is trust and integrity. Trust and integrity are important, not just in living our core values but in being competent in our performance.

Expectations. Accountable leaders set and manage expectations. They know what and when things need to get done. In business, managing expectations means having the ability to keep the client informed on the status of a project to mitigate possible conflict.

Action. Accountable leaders take action, even when they do not feel like it.

Accountability. Accountable leaders set the example for their team; they set clear expectations and hold team members accountable for their roles.

Having a winner's mindset requires accountability. Personal accountability means being intentional about what we do, what we say, what we think, what we believe, and what we want in life. The same is true for team accountability. I have seen the demise of a promising championship team fail because team members were allowed to get away with poor performance with no consequences. We've heard the phrase, "Hire slow and fire fast." As hard as this can be for an athletic coach or a business leader, they would be well-served to follow this advice to keep the high-performing team members and to waste no time in letting go of the low-performing members. That's the case in professional sports as well. Players or employees are either meeting expectations of their position or they are traded or fired.

When your intention is clear, so is the way.

—Alan Cohen, *The Master Keys of Healing*

Chapter Nine:
Leading with Resilience

Life doesn't get easier or more forgiving, we get stronger and more resilient.
—Steve Maraboli, *Unapologetically You: Reflections of Life and the Human Experience*

When I think of resilience, I think of so many family members, friends, and colleagues who survived challenging times through the 2020 pandemic, the first pandemic in a hundred years—the first ever in most of our lives. There are many definitions of resilience and I've used a couple in previous chapters. For this chapter, I would like to use my own definition of resilience, which is the ability to bounce back from something that could have taken you out mentally. In other words, a difficult situation that, if it had not been for the grace of God, would have been exasperating. I'm talking from experience. I don't know about you, but I have discovered strength through this pandemic that I did not know I had. I have had to dig deep into my spiritual soul for resilience. For me, this was not a period in my life that I was able to weather on my own. I know it was my faith in God that brought me through the darkest nights I have experienced in a long time. It was not only the personal effect of the global pandemic that took me to the valley on some days but also the loss of jobs for many Americans, racial tensions, mass shootings, and political divisiveness in our country. For some, I know the list is much longer. I watched my nephew, a single parent with seven kids, lose his restaurant job during the height of the pandemic. I am grateful to be in a financial position to assist my family in times of need, but many Americans do not have that support. My heart goes out to them.

I shared my humble beginnings with you in an earlier chapter. It took faith and resilience for me to overcome the adversity growing up in Liberty City; and in hindsight, it may have been easier to succumb to the life dealt to me at birth rather than fighting to reach my God-given destiny. Being a role model for my family and others is what kept me going—and keeps me going even today. I am hopeful that, one day, my young great nieces will see me as an example of what being resilient can lead to.

When I think back to Super Bowl XXXIV, the year the St. Louis Rams won, I think of Mike Jones. A linebacker for the Rams, Mike made the biggest play of the game and his career. With six seconds remaining on the clock, Mike made "the tackle"; and just like that, the St. Louis Rams won the Super Bowl. Mike later said he had been exhausted and it took everything in him to make that play. He could have easily given up, but he persevered. And because of his resilience, the Rams won the game.

As great as Jones's play was, it doesn't compare to the resilience I witnessed in a YWCA Metro St. Louis client, who I'll call "Sarah." Sarah lived in our housing program for homeless women. Sarah had survived domestic violence, homelessness, drugs, and jail before coming to YWCA housing program. One day I was at work when Sarah ran up to me in the hallway. She said, "Ms. Bracy, guess what. I am moving into my own apartment for the first time in my life."

Sarah explained to me that she had always lived with someone else before surviving the tough life on the streets. Moving from the YWCA and into her new apartment, along with receiving her GED, starting junior college, and finding a good job making a living wage, she was finally going to be a productive citizen of St. Louis. Sarah's story is what I call "Resilience"—with a capital R. With the assistance of YWCA staff, Sarah had found the help she needed to get back on her feet.

Through Sarah's experience, I learned one major thing about resilience, that is, that adversity does not discriminate. At one time or another, every leader will face adversity. If you have not so far, keep living. I like to call my personal adverse and difficult experiences "journeys" because they do not last forever. In other words, it is not my destination. A journey takes us from one place to another. How we choose to respond to the circumstances of that journey determines our experience.

It is not what happens to you,
but how you react to it that matters.

—Epictetus, Greek philosopher

It is not always easy to have a positive attitude during a journey. It is easier to feel like a victim, to feel fearful, anxious, angry, depressed—and the list goes on. Resilient leaders realize that the fastest way to overcome adversity is to face it head on and control the things they have control over.

During past professional journeys, I struggled with trying to control circumstances that were out of my control. Unfortunately, my attitude negatively affected the performance of my team. That was when I learned about emotional intelligence. We can also call this "self-awareness." I learned as a leader, when facing adversity, that it was up to me to channel my emotions in a way that would motivate my team to continue to work hard even during tough times. *Speed of the leader, speed of the team.*

Resilient leadership inspires, motivates, and shows appreciation to the team, especially during difficult times. My past life experiences of resiliency during difficult times, especially those out of my control, have helped me to lead an organization through one of the toughest times in America's history—the pandemic.

YWCA Metro St. Louis is considered an essential business because of the basic-need services provided to the community; therefore, during the entire pandemic, we could not stop providing services to the community, which demanded the doors of YWCA to remain open. This was very difficult for staff, as you can imagine. The leaders of YWCA rallied together to inspire and show appreciation to staff during these unprecedented times. As of today, the effects of the pandemic have lasted over a year; and even though I no longer oversee them, I am proud of the resilience displayed by the leaders and staff of YWCA Metro St. Louis.

Through adversity not only are we given opportunity to discover our inner strength, we are also given the gift of foresight so we can shine a light for others who go through the experience after us.

—Rachael Bermingham, *How to Market Your Book*

Are we born with resilience or do we develop it? For me, that is not important. I believe that, just like accountability, confidence, and other important characteristics of a strong leader, we can develop resilience if we choose. Yes, I believe resilience is a choice.

As I mentioned earlier in this chapter, I had a choice when I was a young girl. I could take the easy road and live in the negative environment I was born into or I could fight for what I believed was God's calling for my life. As you know now, I chose the latter. I believe the same is true in business. Leaders have a choice to either give up or fight.

A Japanese proverb speaks to the concept of Japanese resilience. It says, "Seven times down, eight times up." My translation: Never, ever, give up. As we say in English, "If at first you don't succeed try, try again."

As a leader, I have been knocked down many times. Each time I got up, I was stronger and wiser. But it wasn't always easy. During those difficult times, I had to demonstrate grit. What is grit? Grit can be defined as having courage, determination, and strength in character. When I think of GRIT, I think of gutsiness, resolve, intuitiveness, and toughness. Grit is being able to weather the storm with a positive mental attitude. It's the ability to stay focused on your goal while things around you may feel like they're falling apart. It's having the intuition and belief that everything will be okay if you don't give up.

Resilient leaders can be developed through a learning process and experience. It has been said that experience is the best teacher. Typically, the more painful the experience, the stronger the lesson. My experiences included being discriminated against because I was Black or a woman or sometimes both. That was when I relied on my faith to get me through the difficult journeys.

Truth be told, I did not always embrace adversity as an opportunity to grow as a leader. Early in my career, there were times when I allowed my emotions to rule—internal, not external, emotions. To clarify, internal emotions project inwardly. For example, when things bothered me on the job and I did not speak up, I experienced internal emotions. I did not want to be labeled as the angry Black woman, so I stayed quiet and internalized my feelings. External emotions focus outside of us, such as when I spoke earlier of the racist or negative gender comments directed toward me or when I allowed other people's opinions and words to influence how I reacted, when anger was directed at another person. And in most of those instances, the external emotions led to bad experiences.

Working in the NFL, I lived by the saying, "Don't let them see you sweat." Unfortunately, I was the only person hurt by internalizing my feelings. I learned that resilience required me to speak up for myself and for justice in light of injustices.

Being Black and a woman was not always easy in corporate America. However, I must admit there were opportunities in my career where being Black and a woman was a blessing, and I took full advantage of those opportunities.

Take advantage of every opportunity;
where there is none, make it for yourself.

—Marcus Garvey, political activist, publisher,
journalist, entrepreneur, and orator

Many attributes describe a resilient leader. My favorites: self-awareness, positive mindset, self-care, excellence, investment in others, strength from loved ones and faith—and, of course, GRIT, as I mentioned earlier. I selected these attributes because they have helped me survive my journeys throughout my life.

Self-awareness ranks as one of my most important attributes in being a resilient leader. I consider self-awareness my thermometer, my gauge; it lets me know when and if change is necessary. In other words, do I need to pivot?

Having a **positive mindset** helps me to stay focused and believe that things will work out, no matter how difficult my journey may seem.

Practicing **self-care** helps me stay balanced during difficult times. Pre-pandemic, I made sure to have a massage once a month. I plan to get back to that once pandemic lockdowns and public restrictions lift. In addition, I meditate, exercise, and eat right as much as possible.

Striving for **excellence**—not perfection—allows me to continually work at self-improvement without beating myself up if things are not perfect.

Resilient leaders **invest in others** to foster trust in their team, as well as to help develop and grow their skills. I have mentored young women for decades, and I get joy from watching them grow, flourish, and become resilient women.

Drawing **strength from my family** and **faith** keeps me grounded and confident, so that no matter what I am going through, I am not alone and things will work out. My family is strong in faith, starting with my husband. My sisters, Geraldine and Ramona, are my prayer warriors. I have talked about my best friend, Melissa, who gives me the encouragement I need when I'm in the valley. I'm fortunate to have a village of wonderful people in my life. As of today, I have several sister tribes: my snap sisters (sisters in my Links, Incorporated Gateway IL chapter); my Pineapple Sisters (women I had the pleasure of joining on a girlfriend's getaway trip in Jamaica); my Sisters4Ever (high school girlfriends); my AKA sorority line sisters; my Rooted Sisters (women's Bible study group); and my SistersInChrist (church girlfriends). There are many, many more family and friends that I turn to when I need a pick me up. Bottom line: surround yourself with people who give you support, strength, and a village.

Now, I would like to introduce you to three women who share their stories on leading with resilience. These women exemplify the essence of resilience. I have had the pleasure of knowing these women professionally and have admired their tenacity and grit over the years.

It is my pleasure to introduce you to Marilyn Bush, president, Bank of America Missouri; Penny Pennington, managing partner, Edward Jones; and Michelle Tucker, president and CEO, United Way Greater St. Louis.

She is clothed with strength and dignity, and she laughs without fear of the future.

—Proverbs 31:25 (NLT)

By Marilyn Bush, president of Bank of America, St. Louis

If resiliency defines how well we deal with and rebound from life's most difficult challenges, navigating the pandemic healthcare crisis will forever leave a lasting imprint on our personal and professional lives. From a leadership perspective, in 2020, the health and well-being of every colleague became "our priority." Whether teammates were asked to work from home or in modified, front-line conditions, the goal of keeping every associate and their families safe was paramount.

By putting human interests at the heart of every decision, the tone was set for a culture of care, empathy, and compassion as the pandemic unfolded. It led to greater followership and trust. Leaders expressing gratitude and appreciation for their teams fostered positivity, improved productivity, connectedness, and a healthy mindset. While these actions during the pandemic brought us closer together, building resilient teams starts in "good times."

Before adversity strikes, leaders who cultivate team confidence set their team up for success. Reminding teammates of their towering strengths, praising often, and reinforcing how their capabilities contribute to the greater purpose build camaraderie and create meaning for the work being performed. Find the bright spots in every day and the silver lining in every situation, frequently communicate a positive outlook. A clear vision of where the team is headed, coupled with unwavering optimism, builds team confidence and the belief that, collectively, we can accomplish anything, especially when managing through the most difficult times.

Jim Collins and Morten T. Hansen, authors of *Great by Choice: Uncertainty, Chaos, and Luck: Why Some Thrive Despite Them All* (2011), shares the importance of team-preparedness training in good times and bad. His parallel of the 20-Mile March points out that being prepared for turbulent times requires training in all conditions, which builds confidence to perform in difficult and adverse situations.

For me, in these times of adversity, reminding the team of their incredible resilience helped get through the difficult moments. Challenges became opportunities. By living each challenging day in the present, the team remained focused, avoiding the worry of the future and regrets of the past. Trust among the team created a stronger bond because a safe, trusting environment had been cultivated. Overcommunicating, with full transparency, kept the team on course and moving forward.

Resiliency is an attribute that leaders purposefully cultivate in their teams. While individual resilience is an important competency, team resilience is an imperative quality to successfully navigate adverse situations. It takes time to build a culture of care, solidarity, followership, and trust; but the end result is a team that has a mindset that will endure the toughest of times, and an organization that is built to last.

By Michelle Tucker, president and CEO, United Way Greater St. Louis

"It was the best of times. It was the worst of times," an adage first written in Charles Dickens's *A Tale of Two Cities*

(1859) and frequently referenced to convey two contrasting situations, also a saying I find appropriate when describing a bittersweet yet defining moment in my leadership journey.

After over a decade of leading internal teams at a Fortune 500 bank, I faced a reinvigorating turning point in my career in 2008 in accepting a new position: a highly visible leadership role, one with a strong focus on corporate social responsibility (CSR) and brand-building efforts within the community. At my time of acceptance, I was nothing short of eager to begin; but less than two months after this promotion, our country faced a devastating financial and housing crisis that would threaten the stability of our economy and every community that depended on it.

Ultimately, this desperate situation warranted governmental support, and relief funding was issued to a variety of businesses under the Troubled Asset Relief Program (TARP). Between widespread panic, frustration, and elevated tensions, the financial crisis required a careful response from major banking institutions—a shift in focus that would change the expectations of my role overnight. Though my new title and its approaching challenges paled in comparison to the life-altering situations many others were experiencing, I found myself knee-deep in one of the most reflective times of my career.

Early responses to the challenging circumstances ranged from establishing vital community relationships and assessing urgent needs to meeting the situation head-on while in communication with protesters, community organizations, nonprofits and their struggling clients. Recognizing the severity of the economic climate and the impacts on real people, I decisively opted for the most direct approach: fully and immediately surrounding myself with those directly affected because their perspectives mattered most and could help inform our next steps to assist.

Though not the easiest path, this decision certainly proved to be the most appropriate; and as a result, cherished relationships and trusted partnerships established during this extremely tumultuous time only grew more reliable. To this day, I regularly connect with these longstanding contacts and networks, as we recognize the value of collaborative efforts in driving stronger responses to the needs of our community. Because of our shared experiences and close collaboration, not only can we vouch for one another's strengths, but we know who to depend on when faced with future challenges.

When I consider the most formative moments of my career thus far, I'm reminded of the words so eloquently spoken by Dr. Martin Luther King Jr. in *Strength to Love* (1981): "The ultimate measure of a man is not where he stands in moments of comfort and convenience, but where he stands at times of challenge and controversy." This sentiment not only inspired me through the financial crisis of 2008 but also as the new president and CEO of the United Way of Greater St. Louis during the outset of the pandemic in 2020, where there was surely no blueprint to follow. With each unprecedented challenge, squarely facing adversity by confronting difficulties head-on, with empathy, has proven to be a highly effective strategy. This approach leaves little room for avoidance and inefficiency, overall helping to strengthen leadership and resiliency.

Considering the widespread devastation of both the 2008 financial crisis and the rapid spread of the 2020 pandemic, I've taken note of the fact that it has seldom been in anyone's best interest to delay a needed response to an issue. At the very least, taking that first step forward enables the opportunity to refocus resources and energies on the prioritized situation as quickly as possible. If anything, forging ahead through these times of immense difficulty has better informed my day-to-day leadership. Feeling confident in the efficacy of my leadership style has only reinforced the immediate responses I gave during these adverse periods, allowing me to be better prepared to take even stronger and more precise action in the future.

By Penny Pennington, managing partner, Edward Jones

Edward Jones celebrates its 100th anniversary in 2022. Throughout that time, our firm has had six managing partners. (As a partnership, we don't have CEOs; we have managing partners.) Of those six, I am the first woman.

It's important to know that while gender does not define my tenure as managing partner, it's something I am certainly proud of. Succeeding in a male-dominated industry is something that Adrian and I have in common—and I'm happy to note that in finance, as well as in football, women continue to make great strides all the time.

Being the first female managing partner in Edward Jones' history isn't the most significant difference between me and my predecessors. Instead, it's the fact that I'm the first managing partner who never met Ted Jones.

Ted Jones was the son of our founder, Edward Jones, Sr., and is the person who built the firm into what it has become today. His influence is still strongly felt in every aspect of our business. He is not just a legend in our firm; he is *the* icon to whom we point for inspiration and an example of what "good" looks like when it comes to character, commitment, and vision. Like everyone at Edward Jones, I'm incredibly grateful to Ted for entrusting us with the firm he built—that we might build it even better in service to millions of clients.

Certain aspects of our firm are evergreen—they've been around since the beginning and are still a part of us today. The one that's most prominent in my mind is our sense of purpose. Edward Jones has always been about more than the business of "making sense of investing." Ted identified underserved markets where he knew an innovative firm could create value and improve lives for people who otherwise would not have had access to the tools to build wealth and prosperity for themselves and their communities. Today, that tradition continues with a purpose rooted in making a positive impact on the lives of our clients, colleagues, and communities.

As a leader, it's my job to set the ambition for what we can and should achieve, and foster the conditions that ensure we will continue to deliver on that purpose for generations to come. At times, that has meant overcoming significant difficulties. When the pandemic arrived in 2020, for example, our 50,000-member team was challenged like never before. But we made a decision—as a team—to never stop serving our clients, supporting our colleagues, or strengthening communities, even when we elected to close our branch offices to the public. We found ways to help those most important to us at a time when they needed us the most.

We couldn't have done that without the beacon of a strong purpose and a clear set of guiding principles in place. We often dealt with incomplete or conflicting information that required us to be comfortable leading without a playbook. It was definitely a bit frightening; it was also the definition of resilient leadership, empowered by our purpose.

In moments like that, I feel a connection to Ted and the way our firm has always been led, from one managing partner to the next. I know in those moments that I'm walking in his footsteps. And my confidence is bolstered every day by those I get to walk alongside as we work in service of others.

There are other times, however, when I know I have to create new sets of footsteps and blaze new trails for our firm. We're in the midst of one of those times right now, in fact. As I write this, Edward Jones is in a period of transformation. We're changing some of the fundamental aspects of our business in order to grow our impact and create new value for those we serve, and to seize the unique opportunity in front of us to reach tens of millions of investors and their families. To grow with purpose.

We're moving more quickly than ever before and engaging with our clients—and with each other—in entirely new ways. The headwaters of our transformation are fueled by our purpose, and our ambition is to grow our impact in ways that our forebears would be proud of and that our current and future clients deserve.

For me, then, the key to leading with resilience is purpose. It creates the foundation on which everything else in a successful organization—and a successful life—is based. And as long as that foundation is rock-solid, you can build a mighty impact on top of it. That's what we've done for 100 years at Edward Jones, and it's what we'll do in our next century—and beyond.

Such inspiring commentary from three amazing and resilient women. Thank you, Marilyn, Michelle, and Penny.

I encourage each reader to realize the strength and resilience you have within; and if you cannot do it on your own, find someone to help you. It is not the obstacle or adversity that keeps us from reaching our fullest potential but how we respond to the adversity. Be resilient!

Resilience is not all or nothing. It comes in amounts. You can be a little resilient in some situations but no others. And, no matter how resilient you are today, you can become more resilient tomorrow.

—Karen Reivich, PhD, Co-Director, Penn Resiliency Project, Research Associate

Chapter Ten:
Lessons Learned

Lessons learned are meant to make us wiser
so that we can share them and help others.

—Adrian E. Bracy

By now you know that my foundation is built on my faith in God. There were times in my life that I would ask God, "Why is this happening to me? What lesson are You teaching me?" Trust me, I have learned a lot of lessons in life. This chapter will highlight some of the lessons I have learned in Chapters One through Nine. It is important to me that you either learned a lesson or two from this book or were reminded of a lesson you have learned throughout your career or life that you can share and help someone else.

Lessons learned recognize the mistakes,
correct and apply them, then write them down and
share them with others.

—Adrian E. Bracy

Lessons Learned from Chapter One: My Half-Time Story

First and foremost, take time in your life for halftime, a time to reflect on what's working and what's not working in your personal or professional life. Today, Americans are on auto-pilot and we keep going like that hamster on a wheel. For some people, the pandemic has slowed things down a bit; but I am concerned that when things go back to our new normal, we will once again return to the busyness. When we become so busy, we don't take time for a self-check and end up burnt out or not performing to our fullest potential. That's what halftime will allow you to do: take time to rest and evaluate your performance. It is better that you do it before someone else does it for you. As Vito always says to me, "Inspect what you expect."

Lessons learned:

- Surround yourself with people who want the same thing in life as you, people who will make deposits in your life not just withdrawals. Remember my high school spa divas? They played an important role in my success today.
- Be open to advice. The Bible says in Proverbs 15:22, "Plans fail for lack of counsel" (NIV). If I had not taken the advice of my college counselor, I would have majored in political science and my career trajectory would have been different.
- Join a professional organization. When you volunteer, do your best as if you were getting paid, then you will reap what you sow. My volunteerism led me to an eighteen-year career in the NFL. Remember, it's not always who you

know, but just as important is who knows you. You never know who's watching you, so always do your best.

- Be willing to take risks. If I did not take the risk of leaving the Miami Dolphins, I would have missed out on going to the Superbowl with the St. Louis Rams and later becoming the first African-American female CFO in the NFL with the Arizona Cardinals. Trust God.

What is your halftime story? What halftime lessons have you learned in your life?

Lessons Learned from Chapter Two: Procrastination – Stop Procrastinating

Procrastination is something that I struggle with from time to time, but I am so much better today than I was five, ten, or even twenty years ago. Maturity has a way of helping us recognize that life is not a dress rehearsal and we do not have time to waste on frivolous things. When I think about all the excuses I gave myself that prevented me from writing this book or accomplishing some of my goals, I realize how much time I wasted doing nothing that brought me closer to achieving my BHAG.

Lessons learned:

- Practice overcoming fear with faith. Listen to the GPS, God's Positioning System! I realize this is not easy but with practice you can overcome fear.
- Overcome doubt with trust. Trust your instinct if it feels right and you have peace about the situation. In the Bible, the book of James 1:6 says, "But when he asks, he must believe and not doubt, because he who doubts is like a wave of the sea, blown and tossed by the wind" (NIV). It goes on to say that people should not expect anything because they are unstable in their thinking.
- Get clarity about your vision and your goals. What will it take for you to achieve your Big Hairy Audacious Goal (BHAG)?
- Create your strategic plan to achieve your BHAG. Once again, use the GPS, God's Positioning System, to help you navigate and give you clear direction.

- Be intentional about achieving your goals. Do not take things for granted that they will just automatically work out the way you planned. Be proactive and go for it.
- Find someone like a coach to hold you accountable. If I had not hired Edie as my coach, I feel strongly that I would not have written this book.

What are you procrastinating about and what action steps will you take to recover from procrastination?

___

___

___

___

___

___

___

___

___

___

___

___

___

___

___

___

___

___

___

Lessons Learned from Chapter Three: Game Plan – Goals, Strategy, Practice, and Execution

Having a game plan with goals and a strategy is great, but that's not enough to succeed. You must execute your game plan and strategy. After execution of your game plan, you must put it into practice to achieve your goals. Can you imagine any sports team going into a game without a strategy to win? Chances are, they will lose the game because they are not prepared. Don't get me wrong. You can still lose a game after you've prepared to win, but at least you have a greater chance of winning with a thought-out game plan and strategy. Coach Mike Martz former Offensive Coordinator for Super Bowl XXXIV Champs St. Louis Rams had an offense game plan like none other; it was certainly different from most coaches. In 1999, Coach Martz shocked the NFL by reinventing a strategy known as "Air Coryell," named after the late NFL coach Don Coryell. In this style of play, the passing game was used more than the transitional running game. I would listen to commentators talk about how teams win games by running the ball, but that's not how Mike Martz played the game. He created a dynamic duo with Isaac Bruce and Torry Holt, the best wide-receiver duo, in my opinion, since the "Mark brothers" during my time with the Miami Dolphins, i.e., Mark Clayton and Mark Duper.

Lessons learned:

- Write down your goals; don't just keep them in your mind. If you don't have the right road map, you may get lost and never achieve your dream.
- Find a trusted friend with whom to share your goals and hold you accountable. Better yet, hire a personal leadership coach to hold you accountable.

- Be flexible with your goals. Be willing to pivot if needed. Always be true to yourself. If your goals change, that's okay. This is your life and you need to be happy. Make the goals yours and not someone else's.
- Consider joining a professional network within your profession like NABA.
- If you're not sure about your decision, ask a trusted advisor or do what I did: pray and ask God for direction.
- Having clarity is vital in your quest to reach your goal. It's difficult to get support from others if you're not able to articulate your dream clearly.

Trust your intuition.

List your game plan for one goal and strategy for achieving it:

Lessons Learned from Chapter Four: Game Time – Do You Have the Right People on Your Team?

My husband is a sales guru. When I asked him what made him successful in his twenty-plus years at the same job, he said, "Hiring the right people." He told me that he had a dream team. Everyone clicked on the same cylinders. They had issues, he said, but they always communicated in a respectful way. They listened deeply and sometimes had to agree to disagree. However, they were on the same team with the same financial goals in mind, which made reconciliation critical to the success of the team. It is important for a leader to celebrate, inspire, and respect each team member. When I first became a leader, I didn't always celebrate the wins of the team. I took it for granted and that was a mistake. When I learned the importance of celebrating my team wins, the morale of the team increased. My team felt appreciated and respected for their work, which fostered more creativity and innovation in their thoughts and actions.

Lessons learned:

- Hire the right people. This sounds easier than it is, but it's critical to building your team. Hire for talent not emotions.
- Hire slow fire fast. If you do not have the right team member, it's better to part ways earlier than later. Remember the old saying: "One bad apple can spoil the whole bunch."
- Face the challenge head on and don't become an emotional hostage by holding on to the wrong person for fear of employee retaliation; for example, an EEOC claim or worse, a lawsuit. In the end, you're hurting yourself, the company, and eventually the team suffers.

- To develop a winning team, the leader should possess integrity, compassion, confidence, great communication and listening skills.
- Provide clear expectations for the team and each team member.
- It's important for the leader to practice self-awareness—one of the most important characteristics of a great leader.

Do you have the right people on your team? If so, what will you do to retain your team? If not, what steps will you take to build the right team?

____

____

____

____

____

____

____

____

____

____

____

____

____

____

____

____

____

____

Lessons Learned from Chapter Five: Time Management –Increase Your Effectiveness, Efficiency, and Productivity

As we all know, time is finite; when it's gone, we cannot get it back. For this reason, we should strive to manage our time to live a life of peace and happiness whenever possible. The Bible says, in Ecclesiastes 3:1, "There is a time for everything, and a season for every activity under heaven" (NIV). In David L. Steward's book, *Doing Business by the Good Book: 52 Lessons on Success Straight from the Bible* (2004), he says that World Wide Technology (WWT), a company which he founded, works hard to save time for their customers by introducing ways to increase efficiency. At the end of the day, it all comes down to saving the customer time. Time management is a key component to winning a football game or achieving company goals. I have wasted so much time doing things that did not bring me closer to achieving my personal or professional goals. I've had to learn a few lessons to help me increase my effectiveness as a leader.

Lessons learned:

- Avoid distractions. I've always worked on more than one project at a time. It's the way my brain is wired. Sometimes that's good and sometimes not so much. As long as I have a strategy to complete the projects, I'm good. It's when I allow distractions like answering a telephone call in the middle of a task or responding to text messages that I lose time and, quite frankly, am less productive. If necessary, hire a time-management coach to keep you accountable.
- Get enough rest! For me to be productive and use my time wisely, I have to go to bed earlier than before so I can wake

up feeling energized instead of being worn out first thing in the morning.

- Get organized. I spent many hours looking for something because I was disorganized. Once I had a place for my items and stayed organized, I recuperated more time in my day.
- Set SMART goals for yourself. Remember, a goal is like having a road map to your destination.
- Prioritize your goals and your activities for your day. Don't just wake up thinking you will remember everything you have to do, because, if you're like me, you will get distracted and not accomplish what's really important.
- Use a calendar to schedule your day. I like to color code my calendar to help me see at a glance what's important, whether it's personal, book-writing, lunch, or—the list goes on. I use red as my color for tasks that are urgent and that must get done in a certain timeframe.
- Schedule a time to check your emails throughout the day. Don't spend every ten minutes checking and responding to emails because you will waste a lot of precious time. You can put "check emails" on your calendar to help you stay disciplined. Self-discipline is an important characteristic to achieving time management in your life.

On a scale of one to ten, where ten is highly skilled, how do you rank your time management as a business leader or in your personal life? Do you need to pivot or make adjustments? Why or why not?

Lessons Learned from Chapter Six: The Three P's – Purpose, Passion & Potential

In March 2012, I was fortunate enough to attend Oprah Winfrey's kickoff of Oprah's Life Class: The Tour at the Peabody Opera House. Bishop T.D. Jakes and Iyanla Vanzant were part of the event where Oprah talked about the principles that guide her life. Oprah and Bishop Jakes talked about the importance of having passion and purpose in our lives. They both talked about passion may not pay the bills right away; but if your passion is aligned with your purpose, the money will eventually follow. That may or may not be true for everyone but it was for me. In addition to my passion aligning with my purpose, I also had the potential or skills to achieve my purpose. That purpose was fulfilled by being named CEO of YWCA Metro St. Louis, whose mission is eliminating racism and empowering women. The mission of YWCA aligns with my purpose of inspiring and enhancing the lives of women and girls.

Lessons learned:

- Know your passion and purpose. What's your WHY?
- Operate within your strengths. If you're not sure, try taking a strength-finder survey. There are many resources online. During a coaching course at the CaPP Institute (Coaching and Positive Psychology) with Valorie Burton, I took a survey that gave me my five top strengths. All five were right on target for me, but the top two were spirituality and analysis.
- As you discover your purpose, make sure it is aligned with your potential. In other words, make sure you have the skills to accomplish your purpose in life.

- Write down your personal mission statement and compare it to your company's mission statement; whether you are an entrepreneur or an employee of an organization, they should be aligned. If not, you need to evaluate where you are in your career.

What is your purpose in life or your WHY? What are you passionate about? What is your personal mission statement?

Lessons Learned in Chapter Seven: Having a Winner's Mindset

I believe developing a winner's mindset is a choice. Each halftime decision I've made in my career was a choice. We all have choices in life, and it's up to us to make the right or best decision for our careers. As I shared with you in other chapters, I grew up feeling insecure as a child and young adult because of my humble beginnings. Fortunately for me, playing sports helped me to develop a winner's mindset in high school. I then went on to college where I worked my entire four years as a coop student in the athletic department, which is similar to an internship. Having grit as an athlete is critical to success on the field. Grit is not giving up when we've been defeated. Instead, we push past our pain, get up, and try again. The same is true in business and life in general. My faith is my foundation for having a winner's mindset. My faith gives me hope even when things don't make sense or when things are not going as planned. Some of the characteristics of a leader with a winner's mindset are confidence, persistence, and resilience to name a few. Fortunately for me, I made a choice to develop these and other characteristics needed to have a winner's mindset.

Lessons learned:

- Develop characteristics or traits that breed a winner's mindset, such as setting goals, having self-awareness, building self-confidence, resilience, and self-discipline, to name a few.
- Develop a positive mental attitude. I know from experience that there are mental, physical, and spiritual benefits from positive thinking.

- If you are not sure of your goals, hire a business or life coach. Don't be afraid to hire a therapist if needed. We fail for lack of counsel.
- EmBrace the greatness within you so you can inspire others to do the same!
    - Empower yourself to be great.
    - Move forward – Take action, do something.
    - Believe in yourself.
    - Resilience – Don't give up.
    - Accountability – Do what you say you are going to do.
    - Courage – Step out on faith.
    - Evaluate – Monitor your progress and be flexible.

What does a winner's mindset mean to you?

____

____

____

____

____

____

____

____

____

____

____

____

____

____

Lessons Learned in Chapter Eight: Accountability – No Excuses

It's not how you start the game but how you finish the game that's important. When I think about this statement, I think about the 2008 Super Bowl when the underdog New York Giants won over the undefeated New England Patriots. As a former athlete—well, not really an athlete but a former high school track-runner—I never wanted to disappoint my team, so I always gave 100 percent. That's being accountable to your team. Winning teams hold each team member accountable. The same is true in business. Creating an accountable work environment builds trust within the team. Being accountable is a choice. The good thing is that accountability can be developed, but it requires being intentional and taking responsibility of one's own actions for the good of the team. Having a culture of accountability creates a happier work environment. There are certain non-negotiables everyone has, whether personal or business. As a leader, some of my non-negotiables are integrity, trust, commitment, compassion, and communication. Of course, there are many more non-negotiables but these are the top qualities I practice every day.

Lessons learned:

- *Speed of the leader, speed of the team.* Be an example of an accountable leader. Accountable leaders develop accountable teams.
- Accountability requires self-discipline. Self-discipline helps you to stay focused on the task at hand. Keep your word and do what you say you will do.
- Take ownership of outcomes. Accountable leaders take responsibility of the team outcomes, whether good or bad.

- Make sure employees' values are aligned with the company's values. The benefit could be employee retention, increased productivity, and a happier work environment.
- An accountable leader should have self-awareness. Having self-awareness allows you to recognize your strengths and weaknesses and pivot if necessary.

What are your non-negotiables?

Lessons Learned in Chapter Nine: Leading with Resilience

At some point in life, most if not all people will experience adversity or a difficult situation. The pandemic affected everyone in the world; 2020 was a year we will never forget. Resilience helps people recover quickly from these adversities and challenges in life, including the pandemic. Not everyone in life has the good fortune of growing up around resilient people. Fortunately, everyone has the ability to learn and develop resilience. You've heard the riddle, "How do you eat an elephant? One bite at a time." Resilience is the same way. It doesn't develop overnight; but through practice, time, and intentionality of thought, behavior, and action, you will develop resilience. Resilient leadership inspires, motivates, and shows appreciation to the team, especially during difficult times.

Lessons learned *(including comments from contributors, Marilyn Bush, Michelle Tucker, and Penny Pennington):*

- Keep a positive mental attitude during adversity.
- Before adversity strikes, cultivate team confidence, remind teammates of their towering strengths and praise them often.
- Find the bright spot in every day and the silver lining in every situation.
- Face the challenging situations head on.
- Create a strong purpose and set clear guiding principles for your team.
- Create new footsteps and blaze new trails.
- The key to leading with resilience is purpose. Create the foundation on which everything else in a successful organization and a successful life is based.

In what situation(s) have you had to show resilience? How did you overcome?

Conclusion

Embrace God's greatness within you so you can inspire others to do the same.

I hope you enjoyed reading *Halftime: Learn to Pivot as a Leader and Identify Your Next Step*. It has been a pleasure and joy sharing my experiences and wisdom with you. I am passionate about helping others grow and develop into great leaders. I have not always been the best teacher but, like some of you, I am a work in progress. I strive to get better every day.

One proven way I've used to help grow and develop leaders is through encouragement. My mother, Dorothy, encouraged me to always do my best at whatever I do and to encourage others to do the same. We can do this through mentoring, coaching, or sponsoring someone. I think back to my first mentee, Kenyatta, an intern for the St. Louis Rams. She reached out to me for mentoring. I told myself I was too busy and couldn't take on this task. She persisted, though, and I gave in.

Mentoring Kenyatta was the best thing I could have done for her and for myself. It's been over fifteen years, and I could not be prouder of Kenyatta. Today, she is married with two lovely boys and has a flourishing and successful career—and I'm reaping the benefits of encouraging, motivating, and uplifting her. She is now mentoring me on how to use social media. Truth be told, I would have mentored Kenyatta even if there were no reciprocal benefits. When I encourage others, I am motivated and I feel good about making a positive difference in someone's life. In addition, I feel a sense of happiness and well-being.

Encouragement goes a long way! The 2020 pandemic created a wave of encouragement. To this day, two or three times a week, I'm either encouraging someone or being encouraged, myself, by a family member or a friend. I have witnessed the positive impact I made on a staff member by sharing words of encouragement. Their attitude changed. They became more confident and willing to take risks, knowing they would not be reprimanded for making a mistake. Instead, they would be encouraged to try, try again. They became more accountable and motivated to reach their fullest potential.

I encourage you to pass along this book to a leader or someone aspiring to be a leader. Find someone to encourage today and make it a practice. You will reap many benefits in your life. Stay encouraged!

Blessings and love,

Adrian

Works Cited

"11 Winning Strategies for Overcoming Procrastination." *Indeed Career Guide*, n.d. https://www.indeed.com/career-advice/career-development/overcoming-procrastination. Accessed 25 Aug. 2021.

Bernstein, Gabrielle. *You Are the Guru: 6 Messages to Move You Through Difficult Times with Certainty and Faith*. Audible Audiobook, Audible Originals, LLC, 2020.

Burton, Valorie. *It's About Time: The Art of Choosing the Meaningful Over the Urgent*. W Publishing, 2019.

Chapman, B., and R. Sisodia. *Everybody Matters: The Extraordinary Power of Caring for Your People like Family*. Hamish Hamilton, 2016.

Chen, Robert. "The Real Meaning of Passion." *Embrace Possibility*, 21 Mar. 2015, https://www.embracepossibility.com/blog/real-meaning-passion/.

Collins, James C., and Morten T. Hansen. *Great by Choice: Uncertainty, Chaos, and Luck: Why Some Thrive Despite Them All*. 1st ed, HarperCollins Publishers, 2011.

Covey, Stephen R., Roger Merrill, and Rebeca R. Merrill. *First Things First: To Live, to Love, to Learn, to Leave a Legacy;* 1. Free Press Ed, Free Press, 2003.

Covey, Stephen R. *The 7 Habits of Highly Effective People: 25th Anniversary Edition*. NY: Simon & Schuster, 2013.

Definition of Passion. https://www.merriam-webster.com/dictionary/passion. Accessed 25 Aug. 2021.

Definition of Potential. https://www.merriam-webster.com/dictionary/potential. Accessed 25 Aug. 2021.

Definition of Purpose. https://www.merriam-webster.com/dictionary/purpose. Accessed 25 Aug. 2021.

Dickens, Charles. *A Tale of Two Cities.* 1859. Chapman & Hall.

Dude Solutions, Inc. *Virtual Professional Development: Emotional Intelligence Overview.* https://events.nau.edu/event/virtual-professional-development-emotional-intelligence-overview/. Accessed 25 Aug. 2021.

Farmer, Jill. *There's Not Enough Time…and Other Lies We Tell Ourselves.* Cork: BookBaby, 2012.

Gallup, Inc. "In U.S., 40% Get Less Than Recommended Amount of Sleep." *Gallup.Com*, 19 Dec. 2013, https://news.gallup.com/poll/166553/less-recommended-amount-sleep.aspx.

Geller, Lois. "The Power Of Passion." *Forbes*, https://www.forbes.com/sites/loisgeller/2013/09/27/the-power-of-passion/. Accessed 26 Aug. 2021.

Gregory, Lawrence. "Microsoft's Mission Statement & Vision Statement (An Analysis)." *Panmore Institute*, 13 Sept. 2016, http://panmore.com/microsoft-corporation-vision-statement-mission-statement-analysis.

King, Martin Luther. *Strength to Love.* 1st Fortress Press ed, Fortress Press, 1981.

Lencioni, Patrick M. *The Five Dysfunctions of a Team: A Leadership Fable.* Jossey-Bass, 2013. Open WorldCat, http://rbdigital.oneclickdigital.com.

Maxwell, John C. *Put Your Dream to the Test: 10 Questions to Help You See It and Seize It.* Thomas Nelson, Inc., 2011.

Maxwell, John C. "Borrowing Experience." John Maxwell, 6 Oct. 2011, https://www.johnmaxwell.com/blog/borrowing-experience/.

Plummer, Matt. "How to Spend Way Less Time on Email Every Day." *Harvard Business Review*, Jan. 2019. *hbr.org*, https://hbr.org/2019/01/how-to-spend-way-less-time-on-email-every-day.

Meads, Kate. "Procrastination – the Art of Avoidance." https://www.linkedin.com/pulse/ procrastination-art-avoidance-kate-meads. Accessed 25 Aug. 2021.

"Purpose Definition | What Is Purpose." *Greater Good*, https://greatergood.berkeley.edu /topic/purpose/definition. Accessed 25 Aug. 2021.

Silverstein, Sam. *Non-Negotiable: The Story of Happy State Bank & The Power of Accountability*. Sound Wisdom, 2015.

Steward, David, and Robert L. Shook. Doing Business by the Good Book: 52 Lessons on Success Straight from the Bible. 1st ed, Hyperion, 2004.

"Time Management." Corporate Finance Institute, https://corporatefinanceinstitute.com /resources/ careers/soft-skills/time-management-list-tips/. Accessed 25 Aug. 2021.

Tyndale House Publishers, editor. Holy Bible: New Living Translation. Tyndale House Publishers, 1996.

Tyndale House Publishers, editor. Life application study Bible: New International Version. Tyndale House Publishers, 1984.

"Vision Statement." *Wikipedia*, 13 Apr. 2021. *Wikipedia*, https://en.wikipedia.org/w/index.php?title=Vision_statement&oldid=1017502178.

About the Author

Adrian E. Bracy, MBA, CPA, is an author, leadership and personal coach, consultant, and inspirational speaker. She is also the retired Chief Executive Officer of YWCA Metro St. Louis where she served for nearly 12 years.

After spending 18 years in senior financial management with the National Football League, Bracy transitioned to the non-profit sector to follow her passion—that is, "to inspire and make a difference in the lives of women and girls." Immediately prior to moving to the YWCA, Bracy held the position of Chief Financial Officer for the Arizona Cardinals. Prior to the Cardinals, she spent more than a decade with the St. Louis Rams. Bracy began her NFL career with the Miami Dolphins/ Joe Robbie Stadium in her hometown, Miami, Florida.

In July 2021, after more than 35 years in the corporate and nonprofit worlds, Bracy transitioned to the next chapter in her career, that of entrepreneur, by launching her coaching and consulting firm, Adrian Bracy & Associates, LLC, DBA The Bracy Group. As a coach, consultant, and speaker, her mission is to help women leaders embrace the greatness within as they inspire others to do the same. Her vision is, "All women will achieve their fullest potential."

As an author, Bracy complements her new career in her book, ***Halftime: Learn to Pivot as a Leader and Identify Next Step***, which fosters leadership skills for women.

Bracy has co-authored several books including, ***Come To The Table,*** by The Rooted Sisters; ***Owning Your G.R.I.T***. by Jennifer Bardot & Carrie Burggraf; ***HERstory: St. Louis Words***

of Wisdom to My Younger Self, by YWCA Metro St. Louis; and ***On the RISE, Volume 2***, by RISE Collaborative.

Bracy has received numerous awards throughout her career, including: Black Enterprise 50 Most Powerful Blacks in Sports; Black Enterprise 50 Most Powerful Women in Business; St. Louis Business Journal's Most Influential Business Women; St. Louis American's Non-Profit Executive of the Year; National Council of Negro Women Legacy; YWCA Leaders of Distinction; Women of Distinction, Missouri Athletic Club; and the Small Business Monthly Top 100 St. Louisans to Know to Succeed in Business.

Let Adrian help you get unstuck and reach your goals! Follow @adrianbracy on Facebook or LinkedIn, and @Bracy4Women on Twitter. Visit her website at www.adrianbracy.com.

Made in the USA
Monee, IL
24 July 2023